UNFORGETTABLE

PATRIOTS OF COURAGE

TRIBUTES TO FIRST RESPONDERS

Eileen Doyon

Patriots of Courage

Published by October Hill, LLC
www.unforgettablefacesandstories.com

Layout and cover design by
Kirsten Larsen Schultz | Marketing Ally
www.marketingally.net

Printed in the United States of America.

ISBN-10: 0692163867
ISBN-13: 978-0692163863 (October Hill LLC)

DEDICATION

I want to tell you about a very special lady, Alice Savasta. She passed away this year on June 18th. She and her husband, John, were friends with my parents. Her daughter, Laurie, is one of my best friends and was my Maid of Honor at my wedding.

Alice was the sweetest, kindest, woman and always was there to help you and her community. She wrote in two of my books. She wrote about her dad who started the Fort Edward Rescue Squad in Fort Edward, New York. She was so very proud of him and would tell me stories of her mom who took the emergency calls and how they evolved.

Alice always supported me and would tell me how proud she was of me. I would stop in and visit with her from time to time when I was in New York, and she would tell me another story. I received an email from her on April 3rd this year, telling me how she started her tribute to her late husband while he was serving our country at war. She wanted to have it published in this book.

Well Alice, your tribute did not make it to this book, but your heart and soul did as always. This book is dedicated to you.

Love you Alice, and thank you for all your kind words and encouragement throughout my lifetime......

CONTRIBUTORS

In line with our mission of Your Story Told by YOU, this book is written by the above contributers in their own words and style. To keep the stories true to their original submission, editing on the stories is limited.

UNFORGETTABLE FACES & STORIES

PATRIOTS OF COURAGE

TRIBUTES TO
FIRST RESPONDERS

This book is a tribute not only to actual First Responders, but includes family members of, friends of, people who have stepped up to help and support First Responders.........people who have become Patriots of Courage
-Eileen Doyon

AMANDA COLEMAN

Irish Angel

My name is Amanda Coleman. I come from the city of Dublin in Ireland. I have family here in Ireland who are in An Garda Síochána who are the police force within Ireland. The love for Blue was very close to my heart.

In Ireland there was a massive protest across the country about water charges. While these protests where going on there was a lot of hatred and abuse toward our police force. Not just from the public but from higher up within the force. It was like the government was against them and the public. The world had become so PC that it is so difficult for them to do their job right. I was outraged by the situation as the Garda who work the streets were being threatened at home and within their stations. It was just awful to watch.

In Ireland you cannot speak out about our Law Enforcement. I found this so frustrating and upsetting. So, I spoke with a family member who is a LEO and he explained to me that the war on LE within the United States was far worse. He explained to me about the cops being shot week in week out. I couldn't believe what I was hearing. So, I went online and researched it all. I was absolutely horrified by the whole thing.

I would watch the funeral processions and the pain and grief of their families and loved ones. It was so heart breaking to watch. But then I see something that really touched my heart and made me realise that there was a love like nothing I had ever seen before. It was a love of a Brother\Sisterhood which stretched beyond miles and miles. I would see officers from all over the States attend the funerals of their fallen brothers and sisters. Whilst such a sombre, sad occasion, seeing a sea of Blue stretched for miles and miles along the procession was extremely comforting to see. To know that the fallen Heroes family would always have their Blue Angels to watch over them.

The fact that the support didn't end there was so wonderful. I watch a whole family of officers, turn up to take a fallen heroes' child to their first day of school, or walk their daughter up the aisle or have their first dance with them. Even come to finish a tree house that their brother in Blue never got to finish showed me the bond of the Blue Family was something that nothing could break.

It was a whole series of things for me that drove me forward to where I am today. Some good and some bad. The bad being the war on cops, watching them being ambushed in their cars or shot on a routine traffic stops to the lack of support from the government, the whole political correctness which limits them in doing their jobs properly, the hate organizations, the lack of respect toward them from their communities. But what got me the most was the amount of suicides within the Law Enforcement community due to PTSD. The very thing that we the civilians don't think about police officers or First Responders having. It really upset me the most. I couldn't comprehend it. 140 LEO lost their lives to PTSD in the last year. At the end of the day these brave men and women took an oath to serve and protect no matter what or who they are called to. A lot of the time there is hatred towards them, but regardless they will always turn up to help.

A police officer or first responders fight is never over when they go home and take off their uniforms. No one knows the impact of what they may have witnessed that day out on the field. Or how it might play on in their minds and play just as heavy on their hearts, so much so that they felt they couldn't go on, it truly is heart breaking.

Then I see the good. Seeing the human behind the badge, the families behind the officers, and the love for Blue within Blue. The fact that they leave their families to keep ours safe and risk their lives and their families' happiness for us is truly a remarkable thing that many could not do. So, I felt although I was thousands of miles away I needed to show love and support towards these every day Heroes.

I knew morale was low as the hatred was becoming like an epidemic through the country. I wanted them to know that they weren't alone, that there was love and support out there for them. To show them their work was not in vain. I was on a mission to do just that. I took to social media and started sending out messages of support and love. In doing so my following grew overnight by Law Enforcement agencies from all over the world. Messages of thank you were flooding my inbox daily. It really touched me as I had no clue it would mean so much to so many. Then I noticed more people following suit. It was refreshing to watch the support grow daily among social media.

I was sent two very awesome gifts from very decorated LE which shaped my journey to date. The first was from Division Chief of DHS Stephen Brooks. It was an honorary SWAT callsign from HRT OPCON-1 which was "Irish Angel" and with that Irish Angel was born. The other was a certificate from Chief of Chief's of police Chief Timothy Griffin. He and the Chief of Chief's did me the great honour of dedicating their St. Patrick's Day to Irish Angel for all the support and love shown the world over for Law Enforcement. This showed me that what I was having such a positive impact within a very close nit community. They welcomed me into the family with open arms and I am most humbled for that.

Along my journey I have met amazing people along the way, some of which are huge inspirations to me, who have now become amazing friends and almost family if you will. One of which is my very dear friend Banning Sweatland. Almost two years ago Banning contacted me and asked me to help him get some posts out within the Law Enforcement, First Responder and Military communities. He told me his vision and I loved what it was. Banning is a former Marine (now LEO) who has a vision to enable Law Enforcement and First Responders to have world class tactical and active shooter training against terrorism in an affordable way. First Responder communities don't have the income to cover what it would cost for this type of training. He also wanted to unite Law Enforcement and First Responders in training as there can be no terrorist situation left to chance. Everyone needs to know how to react in synchronicity so there can be little or no room for error when it comes to keeping communities safe and each other. Banning had contacted me at a time when the terror attacks were happening around Europe and I felt if I could help in anyway then I would. I was only too happy to come on team Emergency Operations Proving Grounds. Not only do we help with the war on terror but E.O.P.G is building a facility on our 36.000-acre site for to help with all forms of PTS, which is something close to my heart. We are also building a facility that will help Veterans transition and help in finding them great jobs and support. I am extremely honoured and privileged to be apart of something that will play such a significant role in keeping our world safe. I will be coming to Texas to work with E.O.P.G soon. If there is one thing Banning has taught me and that is "never give up on your dreams."

The second person who inspires me daily is Kyle Reyes who has now become a dear friend too. His plight to speak the truth and support

Veterans, LE and First Responders is remarkable, and he is unstoppable in his endeavours. He takes no prisoners when spreading his message of positivity and encouragement to Veterans, Police and First Responders. It is truly a powerful thing to see someone take a stand and say what we in this community are thinking. Kyle is the voice for so many. He and Banning are the type of people who act, real go getters to fight the good fight. Kyle, Banning and an awesome team are working on an amazing project to keep our children in schools safe. Which is called "Operation Innocence." They are two of the most incredible people you could meet and I'm proud to call my friends.

Everything that I have learnt along the way through my work for E.O.P.G has thought me not only about the Law Enforcement community but Firefighters, EMS, Dispatchers, Military and Security past and present. What I have learned about these brave men and women made me want to help and support them all. So with the love I have for all these awesome people and their loved ones I created what is now "Irish Angel": a support network for all our everyday Heroes and families to come and share their thoughts and opinions in a safe environment, away from all the hate that we see daily toward them online. I felt I wanted to pay it forward to all those who care and protect all that is good in our communities and countries. But also, to have a place where Law Enforcement, First Responders and Military families can have a voice for they are the forgotten Heroes. The ones who hold the line no matter what colour that line may be. They are the ones who pray that their loved ones walk through the door at the end of their shift. They are true Heroes to me for sure.

Only good things can come from Irish Angel now. I have been honoured to be asked by Law Enforcement Today to be the Irish Ambassador for LET here in Ireland. Which will bridge the gap across the Atlantic for our Brothers and Sisters in Blue past and present.

I have a sister who now is an American citizen she lives in the U.S. with her family and you guys protect them and that means so much. I dedicate this to all brothers and sister in Law Enforcement, Firefighters, EMS, Dispatch, Military, Security and the unsung Heroes their families. Thank you from the bottom of my heart for all the sacrifices you and your families make daily to protect mine.

I would also like to dedicate this to a very dear friend who has been an inspiration to me (Ret) Officer Larry Christian, for showing me that no matter how many lows life throws at you, you get up and fight. Staying positive, strong and moving forward wins every time.

I am very honoured and grateful to be a part of such an amazing community the world over. I may not be in Law Enforcement, but they embraced me into the Blue Family and I feel I bleed Blue too. This Irish Angel will always have your SIX.

"Brother... When you raise your shield so will I.

Sister... when you charge the enemy so will I &

If death awaits us, calling his warriors home.

Let me go smiling by your side.

For we are family."

By Amanda Coleman.
Your Irish Angel.

https://m.facebook.com/BlueIrishAngel/
https://www.linkedin.com/in/amanda-coleman-l-i-o-n-bb49aa19/
https://mobile.twitter.com/BlueIrishAngel
https://mewe.com/join/irish_angel

AMANDA M. COLEMAN
"IRISH ANGEL"

HRT   OPCON-1

Be it now known that in consideration for her dedicated and steadfast support of law enforcement officers around globe, be they uniformed patrol officers, criminal investigators, or Special Weapons and Tactics Operators, the unwavering support of Amanda M. Coleman, call sign "Irish Angel", provides the uplifting support needed to continue holding the thin Blue Line in today's trying times.

"Roofish"   "Chip"   "Precious"   "Mudbone"   "Night Latch"

Ashley Dillon

David J Donnell
Dayton Police Department
8/1982 – 1/2008
Police Officer
Father

There are many ways to describe my father: teacher, officer, husband, parent/coach, friend, son, brother, confidant, compassionate, reader. All these words just scratch the surface of the man that touched so many lives. My father was so full of love but he also loved to make people laugh. There were so many occasions where we would need to be careful if we were drinking anything because a punch line was sure to follow causing the drinker to spit it out. David was the kind of person that believed everything could be solved by talking it out, sometimes over a cup of coffee. He was always willing to listen both in his home life and as a police officer. David was a vivacious reader. He loved when he could read a book and then debate the ins and outs with another person. He was a huge fan of the Harry Potter series and The Hobbit/ Lord of the Rings series. He was a great husband and an even better father. He impacted so many lives with his kind demeanor, his ability to listen and his ability to think outside the box. He was so full of life. In 2007 he was diagnosed with pancreatic cancer. I remember him telling me once that after an appointment he came out, and when he turned on the radio, he heard a song that became his new motto for fighting the cancer. Josh Groban's You Are Loved. For those of you that don't know the song, the beginning lyrics are "Don't give up, it's just the weight of the world. When your hearts heavy I will lift it for you." My father heard that song and was filled with hope and strength. He decided to fight and to give cancer a run for its money. He fought for a year and a day before his cancer snatched his life away. He returned to God after a long and hard battle. My family and I can feel him looking down on us and guiding us.

I have many things that I would love to say to my father, but one of the most important things I hope he know is that I loved him, and I am so thankful that I was able to have him as a father. He taught me so much from self-defense to showing me 4 different ways to solve a math problem. He always showed patience with me and no matter how many times I asked for help, he was always there. He is one of the reasons I became a teacher. He was able to break things down in so many different ways. I knew I could always go to him whether I was having problems on my homework to I was hopelessly lost and I had no idea where I was going. I knew I could always go to him, and he would be there. It's one of the things that I miss the most about him. No matter what the problem was, he would listen and help me come up with a solution. I will never be able to thank him enough for always being there for me when I needed him. Every day there is always something that happens that I wish I could talk over with him especially now that I am in a classroom. I wish I could run things by him to see what he thinks and how he would have handled the situation. I know that he is looking down on me. There are times where I can feel his calmness wash over me, and I think, what would dad have done, and it helps me get through the situation. I pull strength from the fact that I know he is still here watching over us, and that he is holding a cup of coffee and a book just waiting to give me guidance. He is in heaven with my father-in-law, Scott Dillon, and they are proud of us and watching over us. They are both eagerly awaiting their newest grand baby, and they will be celebrating with us and continue to be our Guardian Angels.

B. MARK WELSH

My story begins with the birth of a young man in November of 1984 named Daniel. Though I wouldn't meet Daniel until 1988 when I married his aunt, the years I did know him left a lasting impression. Born in the heart of Middle Tennessee, Daniel, like most southern boys, learned to hunt, fish, and commune with nature early in life. He was like many boys his age and shared the same interests as any young boy growing up. More than anything, he loved to be with his grandfather … hanging out, building car models, or just sharing a good laugh. One of the things I can always remember about Daniel is that smile …. it never left his face. While still a young boy, Daniel's mother was diagnosed with cancer. Though she fought a valiant battle for many years, the cancer won in the end and at the young age of 39 she passed on to her higher rewards., Daniel was in his freshman year of high school and decided to live with his grandparents.

One of the things that Daniel had always dreamed of doing growing up was to be a U S Marine. At the end of his high school career, he never hesitated and joined the United States Marine Corps. Though slightly pudgy going in to basic training, he came home after Parris Island as a lean, mean fighting machine. One thing that boot camp couldn't displace was that handsome smile that would melt girls' hearts. His first set of orders as a newly recruited infantryman was to join the war on terror in Operation Enduring Freedom – Afghanistan. The family had a cookout for Daniel a few weeks prior to shipping out. There was plenty to eat and another uncle that had a bluegrass band made the evening even brighter with music. I told Daniel that when he got back from Afghanistan that he and I would have to go to a shooting range to see if the young Marine could beat the old Air Force cop in marksmanship (though I had no doubt that he would win hands down, you gotta keep those jarheads on their toes, ya know). He grinned, definitely willing to accept that challenge.

When Daniel got to Afghanistan in May of 2004, we heard from him a few times in that first month. Mostly he was still confined inside the wire going through orientation and couldn't wait to get out there with his fellow Marines. June 24th is a day that will always live in my mind, it's the day that in 1988 I married my wife to begin our lives together. As we sat down to supper that evening to celebrate our 16th wedding anniversary with a meal that our two daughters had prepared, we were interrupted by the phone. A wailing sister of my wife was on the line crying that we had lost Daniel. We hurried to my wife's sister's house … the grandparents that had raised Daniel through high school and the news was confirmed, Daniel had died in battle, not yet two months since arriving in Afghanistan. Initial stories were sketchy as military based investigations usually are but in the end, we pretty much learned the truth of his last day.

Daniel, his squad leader and another infantryman, had been on an observation post and had just made it back to camp when they realized they had left a piece of equipment. Making their way back to their post, they stumbled across the enemy setting up an ambush for another squad that was due to go through there the very next day. The Marines were caught off guard initially as they were fired upon. The squad leader went down immediately never to rise again. The other infantryman took a bullet close to his spine that left him temporarily immobile. Daniel was gut shot with his inside workings leaking out between his fingers, but still able to return fire. After a 30 minute firefight single-handedly and also while trying to call in medivac for his downed buddies, Daniel ran out of ammo. Sensing the firing had halted from the Marines, the enemy moved in. Daniel could have surrendered at this point but he was a United States fighting military man and surrender was not an option. The enemy at first attempted to take the radio away from Daniel but he hung on and fought back hand-to-hand. They then broke his arm but still did not break his spirit nor his will to fight …. only the point-blank bullet that snuffed out his life could do that.

His body was flown back to Dover AFB and on to Tennessee. The closed casket funeral was with full military honors and many, many of his friends, family, and neighbors lined the streets as his flag draped coffin drove slowly by in the long black limousine. Daniel was buried next to his mother in a small cemetery just a few miles from where he grew up as a boy. I still stop by his final resting place on occasion and make sure there is a flag at his grave. Daniel, I salute the bravest damn Marine I've ever had the privilege of knowing!

Rest in Peace – PFC Daniel McClenney 1984-2004 U.S. Marine Corps

Citation:

The President of the United States takes pride in presenting the Silver Star Medal (Posthumously) to Daniel B. McClenney, Private First Class, U.S. Marine Corps, for conspicuous gallantry and intrepidity in action against the enemy while serving as a Rifleman, Kilo Company, Third Battalion, Sixth Marines, U.S. Marine Corps Forces, Central Command, in support of Operation ENDURING FREEDOM on 24 June 2004. Private First Class McClenney's fire team was part of an ongoing operation to locate and disarm enemy militia in the Konar Province of Afghanistan. While on patrol, Private First Class McClenney's fire team came under intense enemy fire from two different ambush positions. The ambush was intended to support a much larger attack, targeting Marines and other Coalition forces at Firebase Naray. The enemy would have dealt a detrimental blow to Coalition forces had Private First Class McClenney's fire team not reacted in a quick and decisive manner. Private First Class McClenney continued to engage the enemy despite being wounded on the initial burst of enemy fire. After his team leader was killed, he took over radio communications and gave constant situation reports to the firebases and quick reaction force for 30 minutes. Private First Class McClenney aggressively exchanged fire with the enemy while simultaneously requesting medical evacuation for his entire team. With a severe wound to the abdomen and a broken arm, Private First Class McClenney displayed an indomitable fighting spirit as he fought hand-to-hand, until he was mortally wounded. By his bold leadership, wise judgment, and complete dedication to duty, Private First Class McClenney reflected great credit upon himself and upheld the highest traditions of the Marine Corps and the United States Naval Service.

Bridget McFall

In Honor of
Judy Carol Bradley (Hartstein)
6/19/41 - 01/24/18

Judy Carol Bradley (Hartstein) was a proud volunteer EMT in the 1980's for the small town of Lakeville, Indiana. Judy always loved to have fun, enjoyed caring for people and their families. I had the pleasure of knowing Judy because she was my husband's aunt, a wonderful mother, grandmother, and even a great-grandmother. She is missed very much and will always be remembered for her amazing ability to find humor in stressful situations and keeping people positive when it's needed.

Judy was born June 19th, 1941 and she sadly passed away in January 2018. She met her husband Frank Bradley in the early 1960's and they soon after married in 1965. Their daughter Jenny says "They were a true example of how marriage and commitment should really be. They were together 52 years and they always had each other's backs no matter what." They loved spending time with people and playing games like Bingo together. When they had parties and celebrations, everyone was invited and welcomed. No one was ever left out. "The word stranger was just not in Mom's vocabulary," Jenny told me.

Judy's husband Frank drove the Ambulance when they got called out and they had two other women who volunteered as well by the names of Beverly Stanley and Kathy Hipskind. They all became such great friends and spent a lot of time together both inside and outside of their volunteer EMT work. They laughed together and they cried together too. What they all shared in common was that they really genuinely loved helping people. They went through very good experiences together and also really bad experiences together as all first responders do. They took good care of each other and their families.

Judy absolutely loved the Medical Profession, she had a passion for helping people. Jenny remembers, "She was so excited when she became an EMT. I remember she had this red backpack full of stuff she might need for an accident or emergency. I looked through it all the time. I loved when they all got together and talked about the details of their runs! Mom always had that red backpack with her wherever she went, she was such a good person." Jenny grew up to become a Registered Nurse in Indiana, an amazing mother, and in general just a wonderful person because of her parent's influences. Judy Bradley had a great impact on her daughter and her daughter's three children, one of which is already starting into the Health Administration profession at a young age. Judy was a great role model for the younger generations in her family. She inspired people to help others, take good care of others, and always look on the bright side. "They also used to take the Ambulance to the motor cross races on Sundays and I got to go with them! I can remember mom and dad running across the field with a long spine board to take care of one of the racers who got hurt. They were always ready to take care of the racers if they got hurt or went down in a wreck." Jenny said.

She is missed a great deal, but her entire family has her outlook on life and taking care of people because of the way she was. I am sure she is watching over all of them, including her husband Frank and thinking how proud they make her with everything they have been through and the way they have handled it all. They are a tough, yet extremely loving family just how Judy and Frank raised Jenny to be.

That has all been passed down to the younger generations. It has even been passed down and around to the cousins, nieces, and nephews who will always remember her. Her surviving sisters will always remember their kind, loving sister; Judy for the amazing person she was and still is in their hearts. I would have really enjoyed the privilege of meeting their parents and knowing the type of people they were and the kind of outlook they had on life. I am sure they had a great impact on Judy and her siblings.

Judy truly had an unforgettable face and amazing life stories that will never be forgotten. What an incredible person she was. Rest in peace Judy, we love you!

Chel Medlin

Robert P. Searcy
Air Force Served 1955-1976 – Retired as Staff Sargent
My Dad

I have learned over the years to refer to my dad as someone who loved the only way he knew how. I had a lot of resentment for this man over the years, but I had started out as daddy's little girl and followed him everywhere. I was very close to him, so close that I have very few memories of my mother during my early years because I was always with Dad.

My parents married in 1963 while my dad was stationed in Ohio. My sister was born shortly thereafter and dad was shipped off to Thailand during the Vietnam conflict. After his return, my family relocated to an air force base in Georgia, where I was born.

My dad grew up with his three siblings and his mother. His father passed when my dad was seven years old. His mother only having a 3rd grade education lived off government assistance. My father wanted more out of his life, so he had his birth certificate altered to show his age a year older to join the air force. He spent the next 21 years serving our country until health issues forced him to retire. The change in his life as well as other factors such as my mother having a stroke at the age of 36, the death of his mother, and his entering the workforce again, was more than my father could handle and he began drinking. I think my father had a lot of guilt over things that took place during his life but was unable to make amends, such as losing touch with his son from his first marriage. Dad had married at the age of 19, his first wife was only 15 and pregnant. After the birth of his son, the marriage broke up and his ex-wife remarried another military man and left the country with his son. They never saw or spoke to each other again. Whenever I asked about my brother, my father would break down in tears. The pain of losing his son was too much for him to bear.

The liquor bottle and a beer can became my father's best friends. He was a functioning alcoholic. He still managed to hold down a job even after staying up drinking all night. My mother craved attention, even if it was negative. She had her own issues, being a middle child in a very religious family, she became somewhat rebellious during her younger years seeking attention. Getting pregnant out of wedlock and then moving over 800 miles away from her family and friends, she became very dependent on my dad. She never worked or drove a car once she left Ohio. Her health issues, aside, she would instigate arguments with my dad that eventually elevated to physical abuse. My whole world changed in 1977. I went from daddy's little girl to trying to figure out how to protect my mom from my dad's fists.

I grew up in the era of secrets. No one knew what was going on inside our home. We kept these secrets from our neighbors, friends, and even teachers. I faked being sick a lot missing school, so I could stay home with mom, hoping dad would not hit her if I was there. Many times, I came home from a good day at school to walk in to my mom having black eyes and bruises on her arms and legs. My dad went from being my everything to being the man I was scared of. We lived in our own world inside the walls of our home.

My sister was almost seven years older than me. She used to do all she could to make things better for me and shield me from our parents fighting. She moved out and was married by 19. For the next five years it was just the three of us doing the best we could. After I graduated high school, my mother's health declined further, she was no longer able to walk at only 49 years of age. She was eventually sent to a nursing home as she needed 24 hour nursing care. My relationship with my father diminished even further. He was enjoying the single lifestyle staying out all night at the bars and taking no responsibility over my mother. My sister did put her foot down and let him know that he was to remain married to our mom so that he had to keep up his financial responsibility and carrying the medical insurance for her.

My father went on living his life during the next decade. I moved in with my sister for about two years until I could support myself. I tried very hard to still have a relationship with my dad even though it was very strained. During this time, he lost his license to a DUI and I would take him grocery shopping. We had some ups and downs from time to time but we were still family.

My sister had a son and that helped bond my father to her and her family. He adored his grandson and we were able to experience a side of dad from time to time that would amaze us. A side of his personality we either never saw before or was long forgotten.

Dad did eventually get his driver's license reinstated but not for very long. After his next DUI, he did go to AA as part of his sentencing. I remember the first time I was able to actually carry on a full conversation with my dad about his alcoholism. He had seemed so proud that he had been six weeks without drinking and showed me his token that he earned at AA. Growing up in this environment, I had taken on the personality traits of keeping things to myself and not speaking my opinion. I handled things on my own the best I could as any upset in the house always caused drama and fighting. For me to speak my mind to my dad was big. I was finally able to say things to him that I had bottled up for decades. I told him that I really hoped he was able to quit drinking. I admitted to him that I felt as if my dad died when I was 7 years old and was replaced with a complete stranger. I reminded him how close we had been and how much I had looked up to him and loved being Daddy's girl. This conversation ended with him being very quiet as if he was really thinking about my comments. I was very hopeful for his future and for ours. It wasn't long after that I could tell he was drinking again. I knew my daddy well enough to know by small changes in his personality or voice that he was drinking or just hung over. The next time I took my dad grocery shopping, he bought beer. I again had to put aside my fears and speak up to my dad. It took me almost the whole car ride home to get up the courage, but I finally pulled over the car and looked at my dad and said "I love you and that is why I am doing this. I was so proud you had tried to stop drinking and I understand it is hard but I will no longer be an enabler. I will gladly take you grocery shopping or anywhere else you need to go, but from now own, moving forward, I will not take you to buy beer. You will have to figure a way to get it on your own. Again, I love you and this is why I am saying this". He looked down to his lap, quiet, all the while, looking like a child who had just been scolded. All he could muster up as an answer or rebuttal was "okay". He never again bought beer while I was driving him.

My mom died at the age of 59 due to heart failure. She was in the hospital for almost a week when it happened. The doctors had told us there was nothing that could be done to save her. Her heart was too weak. She passed away while in ICU. We were not with her during her last moments as she wouldn't have it that way. It had been the first time in my life that my mother had said to me that she was tired. I let her go in peace. When my dad entered the room, he let out a sound of pure anguish and his knees buckled. I grabbed him and held on to him for as long as he needed. It came to me a few days later that my mother had forgiven my dad for his abuse and still loved him until the end, that I had to forgive him too. From that moment I let go of all the anger and resentment I had for him and realized that my dad loved us the only way he knew how. Was he a good man even though he was an abusive alcoholic?

To answer this, let me say that Dad died only 11 months after mom. He had lung cancer that was not diagnosed until his last days in the hospital. I was able to finally say the words to him that I had not said in almost 20 years "I love you" he was conscious enough that day to hear me and say it back. I felt that he needed to know this before leaving this life that he was loved. My dad was not a war hero, not a great husband or dad, he was only a human with faults like the rest of us. He had his own issues to deal with but unfortunately for him and for us, he didn't know how to deal with them. He loved us but never learned to love himself. My dad loved the only way he knew how.

DANIEL BOLLINE

Tribute to Captain Paul Blake

Let me tell you a short story about a selflessness firefighter and why I believe he is a firefighter's firefighter, Captain Paul Blake. I have known Paul for 23 years now and he has always been a true humble hero to the Miami-Dade Fire Rescue Department. He has been a liaison between Miami-Dade Fire Rescue and local municipalities within Dade county, helping both the department and communities to work together to benefit the citizens. Paul has been a front line officer of rescues and suppression crews during some of the toughest calls in all parts of our county where he earned a reputation for being a smart officer who thinks clearly and always ten steps ahead. Captain Blake has also been an active local 1403 member for many years and is currently our treasurer.

Captain Paul Blake is a humble hero within our department. He has never looked for awards, nor has he looked to receive a medal for doing what Paul considers just his job to do. His award, or medal, is the feeling of helping those in a time of need. What drives him is his passion to honestly make changes for the better and to make a difference in someone's life, or giving someone hope or closure. Being a firefighter myself, there is nothing more rewarding than a thank you from a family member, or the victim themselves, to make you realize why we put in all the hard work and training that we do. That is what Paul takes pride in. In all the years that I have known him, he has never lost that drive, compassion, or professionalism no matter how tired or worn down he may be.

Paul had an idea of a liaison between Miami-Dade Fire Rescue and the cities, townships and villages which reside within Dade County. He took that idea and put it into action back in 2003. The purpose of this program is to educate representatives and the people in the community of exactly what services we have and can provide to their communities. The program shows compassion to the community's wants and needs. It also put a face behind Miami-Dade Fire Rescue to answer any questions that they may have that could impact them either positively or negatively. This program was Paul's baby. It has changed faces since its development, but it is a lifeline to communities as well as our department still to this day.

I was fortunate to have worked some of the most difficult calls with Paul early on in my career. We had a fire call where we were first on arrival - Rescue-7, Battalion 5. Starting a primary search for victims with fire overhead, while suppression crews were advancing an attack line to extinguish a rapidly growing fire. I was green; it was nerve racking. Knowing that the man next to you is trained and battle tested, and that he would lay down his life for you, makes entering that fire, still scary as hell, but a little more doable. Another fire, we call the beast who does not discriminate, and this time it won. Dealing with the emotional devastation that despite all your hard training and knowledge and push on the call, five family members didn't make it. We experienced calls of pinned passengers in car accidents, extracting a live victim, while the person next to them is deceased. I could go on and on of what we saw and have been through, but I will spare you that. What I can tell you is Paul and our crew, put it all on the line every time we go to work. After the really hard calls, Paul was the guy who pulled us all together and got our heads straight again.

In addition to his job as a Captain for Miami-Dade Fire Rescue, he is also currently the treasurer for our local union, Local 1403. He has been and continues to be vocal, forthcoming and passionate about the importance of improvement in working relations with the county. He has been just as passionate about the delivery of service to the citizens of Dade County and anyone who visits. He has spent countless hours away from his family to better our union, our department, and the community. He has held the position of treasurer since 2010, a position that is voted on frequently with Paul always winning the election by a milestone.

Captain Paul Blake is a remarkable firefighter; a humble hero that works and breaths his profession and doesn't look for special recognition for doing so. He is proactive and always looking for ways to improve service and provide more with what we have. Paul is constantly challenging himself and setting the bar higher for, not only himself, but the rest of us as well. I can only hope there are many more women and men in this profession that are like him. Captain Paul Blake is a real life hero that walks among us, and I am so proud, and fortunate, to have shared some of my best, and worst, events on the fire department with a man like him.

DAVE BRAY

Tribute to Fallen Officers

LAST CALL:

When a person makes the decision to become an officer of law he or she is no longer a civilian like you and me...to uphold their title of POLICE officer, they are forced to sacrifice and abandon certain rights that the average citizen holds dear. From that point on they are sworn to serve and protect the good guys from the bad and hold that ever so fragile piece of territory between peace and civil unrest known as "the thin blue line".

As a law enforcement officer, their fundamental duty is to serve the community;
to safeguard lives and property;
to protect the innocent against deception, the weak against oppression or intimidation..
and the peaceful against violence or disorder;
they are also sworn to respect the constitutional rights of liberty, equality and justice for all... That's quite a job and a hell of a lot of responsibility.

Much like the military, they swear an oath, and that oath, right hand raised, is called the Oath of honor

It goes something like this:

On my honor, I will never betray the badge, my profession, my integrity, my character, or the public trust. I will always have the courage to hold myself and others accountable for our actions. I will always uphold the laws of my country, my community, and the agency I serve.

As a civilian, Does your job or occupation require you to take that oath in order for you to make a paycheck?…
I didn't think so.

Over the years, too many Police officers have died to uphold that oath.
They were mothers and fathers, daughters and sons, community leaders

and coaches and mentors... They didn't give their lives protecting their own personal families and belongings... They gave their lives by doing their job... protecting each and every one of us and holding that ever so precious "thin blue line"

When I first heard a "last call" for a fallen police officer going over the airwaves, I was truly moved. To hear the quivering voice of the female dispatcher trying her best to hold it together practically brought me to tears. Each time she called the badge number of that officer that was killed in the line of duty, a deathly silence and almost tangible darkness blanketed the airwaves. You could literally feel its emptiness.

The words to one of my songs was written in response to the calls of that heartbroken dispatcher...they were written in 3 parts to fill those 3 spaces of black silence that inevitably fall upon the airwaves each time a dispatcher is tasked to call the badge numbers of the fallen. They were written to represent the final words of a fallen officer giving their last requests over the radio...

To his/her spouse... To his/her children...
And to his/her brothers and sisters in arms.

As you listen to the song, I would like you to remember that if that "thin blue line" should happen to crumble and fail then the daily sacrifice and eternal commitment of protecting Yourself, Your loved ones, and all that You hold dear will very, very quickly become your own...

Respect the badge...
Dave Bray

Dave Bray is a United States Navy Veteran. He served in the US Navy as an 8404 FMF Corpsman for the 2nd Battalion/2nd Marines, (Sniper PLT), stationed out of Camp Lejeune, NC.
Dave is now a full time touring musician, singer and songwriter.
Dave performs all over the country and has dedicated his musical career to supporting U.S.Veterans, Active Duty Military, Fire, Police and First Responders.

"Stay the Course..Finish the Fight... & Never Surrender!!!"
-Dave Bray USA

Last Call
https://www.youtube.com/watch?v=AZZAQ5TStaU

http://www.DaveBrayUSA.com
https://twitter.com/davebrayusa
https://www.youtube.com/user/SOVEREN777
https://www.facebook.com/davebrayusa/

DAWN MCCOY

Rich McCoy
FDNY
1/17/90 - 9/6/02
Firefighter
Husband

Rich grew up in a home that nurtured everything to do with family. It was a home of honesty, respect, laughter, hard work, ethics, volunteerism and a tremendous amount of love. It was a childhood filled with family dinners, little league games, Sunday Mass and summers playing manhunt. Rich took great pride in having a backyard that was the sports capital of the neighborhood - until a garden was strategically placed right in the middle of the outfield.

Rich's father, Bill, was a Lieutenant for the NYC Fire Department and his mother, Nancy, stayed home to care for Rich, his brother, Will and his two sisters, Eileen and Kathy. It was a loving childhood that formed the type of husbands, wives, mothers and fathers they would become. I believe there is no greater gift a parent can give their children than to model a life of love, devotion and respect for one another, which is not to be confused with a marriage or life that is perfect.

Rich dedicated his life to public service, first as a NY State Trooper with Troop F in Monroe and then as a New York City firefighter with Ladder 49. Engine 68/Ladder 49 is best known for being the first responders to Yankee Stadium. Rich would often reflect fondly on those years, having worked with many great men. From the times of laughter and camaraderie on the job, to the very real and daily dangers, there was a rare bond that connected all of them so deeply. Rich remained close to these brave and loyal brothers long after leaving these jobs.

I first met Rich 26 years ago when he was a young, polite, confident and incredibly handsome NY State Trooper. We spent a few hours talking about mutual friends, but, they say God has a plan and that wasn't our time to start our life together. I had moved away and 5 years later, while home for a family visit, I stopped to watch my Dad and brothers' softball game and there he was! As fate would have it, Rich played on their team and, at that moment, I knew with everything in me, it was time to start our life together. And we did. 21 years later, we would spend our weekends watching our children play sports on the very same field we met on August 18, 1991.

Being a dad came so natural to Rich. From the moment our children were born, he had an innate sense of calm that he seemed to transport from his heart to theirs as they would lay on his chest. It amazed me how they would settle there for hours, so peaceful and so deeply connected by his warmth, love and safety. I can't imagine a better place in the world to be. This quality in him wasn't exclusive to our children, Rich was adored by his many nieces and nephews and was known as the "baby whisperer". He could often be found with a niece or nephew on his lap looking up into the trees to spot birds and listening to the sounds of nature. Rich shared his love of nature with all of his nieces, nephews and godchildren, I believe this is a gift they all carry with them today. A part of Uncle Richie.

When I think of the morning of 9/11, I remember Rich heading upstate with some of the men from the firehouse. I received a call early in the morning saying they were called into work. He kept the conversation brief and vague and simply told me I needed to meet him just off the highway with a flashlight and to please bring Christy Ann (4), Tara (2) and Patrick (8 months) with me. I sensed an urgency in his voice and immediately packed up the kids. He jumped out of the car and made sure to hug and kiss each one of us before quickly getting back on the road. After getting home and seeing the news, I knew immediately this meeting wasn't about the flashlight, but more Rich needing to see his children before heading down to the firehouse. He did not let on his fear at the time, but, it's clear Rich and these men and women who were called upon, didn't know if they were coming home.

I did not see Rich for almost a week, and after that it was sporadic for the next few weeks...and then came the funerals. There were so many, it felt like every day. Sometimes 2 or 3 in one day. I just can't imagine the daily heartbreak and pain of seeing the devastation left upon these families who suddenly woke up to a life that had been decimated and was now unrecognizable to them. To then compound this with the rescue workers own grief of losing so many close to them, I wouldn't know where to find a continuance of strength every day, but they did. What I saw, in my limited exposure, was layers upon layers of grief, sadness, and anger but, also a strength and determination to keep going and to be there for each other, in ways no one else could. The Brotherhood.

Almost immediately after 9/11, Rich started having health issues, with shortness of breath being the most concerning. He was told to see a cardiologist and, based on the results of his angiogram, his fire department career had now suddenly ended at the age of 38. This was the first critical turn of events in our lives that we didn't see coming. Rich had always lived an active, healthy life, didn't smoke, rarely drank and had no family history of heart issues. Now he's sitting across the desk from doctors who all seemed to agree the only course of treatment would be open heart surgery. But, before moving forward, Rich knew he needed to be sure this was the only option. He went on to find a gifted and experienced cardiologist, Melvin Weiss, the Chief of Cardiology at Westchester Medical Center, who successfully performed 2 complicated coronary angioplasty surgeries on Rich.

Life from that point on was about being present, being healthy, enjoying the outdoors and nurturing and appreciating time together with our families and friends.

One of Rich's greatest joys was coaching the young athletes in our community. His message was always about character and good sportsmanship, first and foremost, and then came winning. He patiently coached in a way that promoted self-confidence, kindness towards each other and perseverance. He was often heard - and often remembered - for cheering his signature "stick with it kid" from the sideline.

Upon Rich's passing in 2012 of a heart attack at the age of 49, it was quickly realized that the community wanted to honor and continue his legacy. The Richard G. McCoy Foundation was established to celebrate and support students who have shown the level of community service, volunteerism and character that Rich exemplified. This foundation has been immensely successful, which is a testament to the man, husband, father, son, brother, friend and coach he was. I find the way in which Rich continues to give back to the youth and the communities he loved so deeply, truly humbling.

The gift of Rich's love and guidance will always be deeply rooted within us,

along with the memories that will forever be the foundation of our family. No matter how many years pass or where life takes us, I see in Christy Ann, Tara and Patrick that the roots from which they grow will guide them on their journey. These roots are solid, they are healthy and strong, and, most importantly, they were nurtured by a love that was so pure, so deep and timeless. These roots are our anchor and where I'm able to find my own peace and strength. I believe it's where we all do.
Dawn McCoy

———————————

Poem written by Tara McCoy
Written: April 26, 2018

My heart has learned to redefine the word "whole" for itself
and in this new definition, it would not be whole without this hole.
I have never known a consistency or relentlessness equal to the one that is waking up and going to sleep thinking about the same thing every day for 6 years.

https://m.facebook.com/RichardGMcCoyFoundation/

https://cfosny.org/our-funds/scholarships/the-richard-g-mccoy-foundation/

DEBORAH LOUISE ORTIZ

Turning Trauma and Pain into Action

This is dedicated to the most courageous man I know, my husband. This is about him, my family and the power of unconditional love, understanding and education.

My husband Michael served 22 years as a New York State Trooper and worked with the Drug Enforcement task force. He took an oath to protect and serve. I knew his work was very important but what I did not know was the toll his work would take on him mentally.

What most of us do not fully understand is that First Responders must deal with the public during what could be one of the worst moments of these people's lives. First Responders witness many horrific scenes, must notify families about tragedies as the first responders families worry if their loved ones will make it home. They do this every day never knowing what they will face.

Many times, they keep these tragic memories to themselves as it eats away at them and they continue to do their jobs. Eventually, for many the trauma they face and learn to keep locked away and unresolved, becomes more than they can deal with and can result in Post -Traumatic Stress Disorder.

For many years my husband suffered in silence until he could no longer keep it locked up. We had no clue what was happening to him. Paranoia, hyper vigilance, depression and anger all but consumed him. The man I once knew, the man I married was gone and it felt as if I was slowly losing my mind.

This is what my husband and our family has had to deal with for years as a result of his job. It has been a nightmare in every sense of the word. Could all of this have been avoided? The answer is "yes". How could have this been avoided? Through effective mental health training through the departments. Unfortunately, this was not the case for my husband's department and is still not the case for most.

His diagnosis of PTSD was just the beginning of a long and very difficult journey. We not only had to educate ourselves on what was happening to him, we had to figure out how to get him help as we quickly became educated about the huge stigma involved when it comes to asking for help for First Responders in need.

My husband felt that he did not need help and that in asking for help he would be perceived as being weak. This is common in the First Responder culture. Breaking through this barrier was extremely difficult until it became abundantly clear that his life had spiraled out of control and he had to make a choice. Get help or lose his family and himself.

My husband finally received help and we have been working hard to ensure that he and our family can maintain a healthy quality of life. My husband's fight literally for his life left me feeling powerless, hopeless and to be honest angry. I could not understand how these brave men and women who serve us all are not being educated or trained on how to deal with the devastating mental effects that could possibly happen to them.

My husband's fight for his wellbeing, inspired me to do something. I decided to use my anger in a constructive way to help others just like us. Through research we found out that PTSD is a huge problem for First Responders and there was nothing being done to address it. A close friend of mine and my producing partner decided to make a documentary called "Code 9 Office Needs Assistance" to help raise awareness, educate the public and most importantly reach other First Responders and families to let them know that there is hope and that they are not alone. The film project bought us together with an amazing group of First Responders and families who shared their stories in hope to help others. We honor each of them.

The film then brought me together with an incredible woman and we then started a nonprofit called Code 9 Project. We work with First Responders and Families all over the country to help train them how to manage the stress and trauma they deal with on the job.

I started this by writing about how courageous my husband is. Courage is about facing fear and following through anyway. Mike did that as a First Responder every day and learned to face his biggest fear, his demons. Mike had to come to terms with understanding that being a police officer is not his only identity. He is a husband, a father, a friend and human being.

Facing his reality and fears has helped me face mine and for that I am incredibly thankful. I am proud of his service to us all and proud to be his wife. Together we have learned that we are strong, and we can get through anything. He has helped me find my strength to stand up for ourselves and others. We once fought hard to be the people we were before PTSD invaded our lives and we came to the realization that we will never be those people again. Instead we are a better version of ourselves with a great appreciation for life.

To every First Responder and family member, we thank you for your service.

As I reflect on our lives I always find myself thinking about all of the families who have been affected by loving a first responder battling with PTSD. We are one of these families and this is for all the families:

We watched as PTSD invaded our homes and we wondered what was happening.

We watched as our loved one became an unrecognizable person and we questioned our sanity.

We watched as paranoia, depression and hyper vigilance consumed their being and we... prayed for strength.

We watched as they cried in the darkness and we cried when no one was around.

We watched as the nights became their enemy and nightmares their reality and we pretended to sleep during our night watch.

We watched as loneliness, hopelessness and the will to move on replaced our dreams for the future and we cursed those who have turned their backs.

We are the families of a loved one who suffers from PTSD and we will not sit back and watch anymore.

We will stand together to rebuild our lives and allow HOPE and FAITH into our homes!

Website: Code9project.org
Facebook: Code 9 Project
Instagram: Code 9 Project
Code 9 Officer Needs Assistance Documentary Website: Code9film.com

DEBORAH OVELAND

Make Us Humble, True, and Thankful

A couple, a man and wife, who reside deep in the heart of Texas and in my heart, wish to remain anonymous. She is a retired police officer, although, I think once a police officer, always a police officer. He is a chief investigator. They are two uncommon citizens and my dearest friends.

"I need to speak to your guy," I tearfully told my precious friend. She is now an author, speaker, editor, following an accident which ended her career in law enforcement, sparing her life.

"Okay, Debbie," she responded without hesitation.

"I don't know what to do," I explained. "It's my heart again."

"Hello, Debbie." He was on the phone now, calm and steady.

I broke down. I rambled, sputtering my concerns, as he listened, offering occasional words of affirmation interspersed by a question, here and there. I was afraid of the known and more afraid of the unknown. Gradually, over the course of about ten minutes, together, we unraveled the situation and traveled the distance from complex, relentlessness to a foolproof plan.

This is the essence, in my mind, of what First Responders do. They go with you, fearlessly, where absolutely no one else wishes to go. Together you face the "grim reaper." If you are conscious and over-thinking a seemingly impossible situation, they sort through the mess without leaving you in the mess. If you are unconscious, or semi-conscious, they think for you, taking actions, on behalf of your life, to save your life. As an observer, I am in awe. As a survivor, great thanks to First Responders, I am grateful.

This tribute is to a couple of First Responders, a man and a wife, both of whom happen to be the dearest of friends to me. I am forever in their debt, humble, true, and thankful. Amen.

Deborah M. Oveland, RN, MSN, FNP-BC

Board Certified Family Nurse Practitioner
Founder, SpeciaLives
https://makelivesbetter.uthscsa.edu/shpdonate

https://makelivesbetter.uthscsa.edu/Oveland

UT Health
San Antonio

DECHIA BADEAUX

Officer Matthew Gerald
Baton Rouge Police Department
March 14, 2016 – July 17, 2016 E.O.W

To my Unforgettable, Blue-Eyed HERO…
Matthew Lane Gerald dedicated his life to serving his country and community. Upon graduation from Central High School he joined the Marine Corps. He served as a Marine from October 11, 1994 to October 10, 1998. Then went on to serve in the Army from August 21, 2002 to May 13, 2009 as an UH-60L, Blackhawk, Crew chief. He completed 3 tours overseas, with over 1,500 combat, flight hours. This man bled RED, WHITE, and BLUE. In February 2010, Matt and I met at the Spanish town parade. We then got married July 7th, 2012 and gave birth to our daughter, Fynleigh on May 23rd, 2013. As a family of four we continued on our journey, struggling to find our way. I was trying to settle in my new career as a Special Education teacher, as a wife, and mother to two very strong-willed girls. He was struggling in the civilian world altogether, trying to find his place. Searching for his calling. The transition from solider to civilian was a huge struggle For Matt. However, he never gave up, he kept pressing forward. God called him once again to be a servant. He swiftly answered the call and became a police officer for the city of Baton Rouge. He was one of the oldest guys in the 82nd academy class but that didn't stop him from fulfilling his dream and once again serving his community. His decision to join the police force was a life changing decision for our family. That decision brought about many new challenges but made our marriage rock solid and new again. God's grace is such a huge blessing.

July 17th, 2016 my world was turned upside down. The comfort and security I had come to know as your wife was abruptly ripped away from me due to "HATE." I received that knock on the door, that is a police officer's wife worst night mare. The kind of knock that will stick with you and haunt you. The knock that you don't want to answer because your heart and gut already know what is lurking on the other side. Those Six grown men there to deliver the message, or should I say confirm the facts that I had already known because my eyes could see just as everyone else could. It was being broadcast across every news outlet and social media site known to man.

In that moment, I was devastated, scared, pissed and felt the weight of the world on my shoulders. How could this be? You are well trained!! You are a Marine, black hawk crew chief, and a policeman. I cannot do this life without you. I need you. I couldn't wrap my mind around it. My blue-eyed rock was gone. Every sense of stability, comfort, and security I had come to embrace and be grateful for was gone. This was not supposed to happen. You worked the day shift.... It was supposed to be the best shift.... Oh man, how naive I was... It's crazy how life works... my forever, GONE... on a beautiful, Sunday morning all due to "HATE" that filled our city. The realization of living out my wedding vows "till death do we part" took on a whole new meaning. Becoming a widow at 37 years old was never part of "our" plan. Saying good bye was the hardest thing I have ever done. I had no idea how I was going to survive financially, emotionally, physically, nor mentally without you. I was shell shocked, just surviving in the turmoil. Just existing.... Then the Miracle...... You always had a way to make light of a situation.... The lord must like your sense of humor as well. Your persistence paid off with speaking to the boss upstairs. Two weeks after you were called home to be with the lord, Paw Paw Charles, and Emily. I had the surprise of a lifetime. I was pregnant.... Yes, you read that right. In the midst of all I was going thru, I now had to figure out how to raise a third child. I had to laugh to keep from crying.... Our miracle though, Falyn Matthew, aka "Baby Buttons" your first and last-born son, the last and only boy in the Gerald family. The best gift you could ever leave behind. Thank you, Lord, for this precious miracle. I am forever grateful and know I am truly blessed.

Matthew Lane Gerald, my blue-eyed angel...

There are not enough words to speak or enough awards to give that could ever amount to what you deserve. I could never do you any justice, but I will try...

Thank you for loving Dawclyn and I without reservation. I know, I wasn't always easy to love but, you did it with such grace and pride. I appreciate your loyalty and dedication to our family, then and now. I am so sorry I didn't tell you this more. Thank you for never giving up on "us" even when I wanted to quit. You taught me a whole new meaning to dedication and perseverance. "Just because things are tough, you cannot give up." I am so blessed and forever grateful that you chose me to be your partner in crime. It was not always easy, but we fought the good fight. I am your first and only Wife, that babe is something I will always cherish. You could have picked anyone but, you chose me and my crazy life. I'm not sure I will ever understand "the why" but so honored, grateful and blessed you did. I love you so much and miss you always.

I am who I am TODAY because of you. During your time on earth you trained me well. You prepared me and gave me the skills necessary to survive in this cruel world. You taught me to not always trust so easily, being loyal and fighting for what you believe in is so important. You taught me how to accept rejection and that standing alone is okay. Especially when your standing alone because what you are doing is the not popular thing but the "something you believe in." You always practiced what you preached... "always do the right thing even when no one is watching." This advice you gave and lived became guidance when I needed it most. You taught me to fight hard for what I believe in and to serve with all my heart. Don't expect anything from anyone and you will never be disappointed. The biggest lesson of all, LIVE LIFE to the fullest, tomorrow is never promised. Be quick to apologize, never go to bed angry. Tell your kids you love them, always hug and kiss them. Take time to enjoy the small moments even when you're tired because you never know when your time on earth will expire. Slow down and enjoy all moments big or small. You showed me what the heart of a lion looks like…. Thank you!!!!!

I have learned many things from you but most importantly you taught me to LOVE without expectations and with no fear. Live, Laugh, and Love to the fullest, each and every day…. You prepared me to survive my worst days and learn what true brotherhood looks and feels like. You continue to show up when I am in doubt….to comfort me from afar and to support me when I need it the most. Thank you from the bottom of my heart for all that you did and continue to do. I will continue to work hard to bridge the gap between police officers and the people. All while working even harder to do what I can by protecting all officers near and far, any way that I can. The biggest lesson of all, you taught me to LOVE again…

Heroes are ordinary people who make themselves extraordinary!!!
Widow, Dechia Badeaux-Gerald
I love you to heaven and back…
Until we meet again….

GINA ELISE

"Side by Side"

My mother had given me a framed photograph of her late father, my
Grandpa Lou. In this striking photo, taken just after World War II ended,
my handsome grandfather stood proud in his U.S. Army dress uniform,
hands behind his back, with a broad smile, looking happy to be home
again. He was 30 years old. He had entered military service at 26, just after
the bombing of America's Navy ships in Pearl Harbor. My mother told me
how proud he was to have served in the U.S. Army Air Corps as an Army
pharmacist, compounding and dispensing the medications so needed by
America's troops during wartime. Years later, he would take his two young
daughters to the local cemetery on Memorial Day and stand solemnly at
attention to witness the playing of "Taps" and show respect for his fallen
comrades who had given the ultimate sacrifice.

The war in Iraq was entering its third year. I'd been seeing news stories of
severely wounded troops coming home, with burns, amputations, illness, and
post-traumatic stress. Young men and women needed extensive medical care
at Veterans Hospitals and at military hospitals, like Walter Reed. I couldn't
get the images of these service members out of my mind. Many of them were
younger than me, and their lives had been changed forever by these wounds
of war. They were heroes in need of help.

I realized that I needed to do something to help care for our ill and injured
troops returning home to VA and military hospitals. But, what could I do?
I didn't have a medical background. Maybe I could raise funding to help
buy therapy equipment for the new Veterans entering the VA system, as
well as for those older Veterans entering the hospitals, who came from my
grandfather's generation.

"How do people raise money?" That was the question I pondered. I
remembered the calendars I'd seen from so many nonprofit organizations.
I began to formulate the idea for a calendar to be sold to raise funds for
new hospital equipment for the Veterans. What I lacked in money to carry
out this project, I made up for in determination and ingenuity. I wanted to
honor my grandfather's service during WWII, and since I'd always loved the

music and fashions of the 1940's, I would try to create a vintage style pin-up calendar. I was inspired by the beautiful nose art of painted ladies on the WWII bombers and of the lovely photos of Betty Grable and Rita Hayworth, the popular images of "the girl next-door," that helped boost morale for America's troops fighting so far from home.

I purchased wigs of different colors and scoured thrift stores and discount stores for vintage clothing. I contacted a photographer and a hair and make-up artist. I located vintage vehicles whose owners were happy to let me pose with their cars and trucks. I found a graphic artist to design the calendar. The first "Pin-Ups For Vets" calendar was printed in 2007. I raised $5,000 from the calendar sales and donated it to a local VA Hospital, in memory of my late grandfather. I like to think he would have been proud of his granddaughter for her service to his fellow Veterans.

I thought that would be the end of my fundraising project, but to my surprise, people who had purchased the calendar asked me when the following year's calendar would be ready to buy. Fast forward to 2018. This year marks the 12th annual edition of the "Pin-Ups For Vets" fundraiser calendar, and we have just wrapped production on our 2019 calendar! We now feature many female Veterans as models in the calendar! We turn them into WWII-style pin-ups! The project that started out as a one-time calendar is now an award winning nonprofit, honored by Congress and also by America's deployed troops, who have flown 10 U.S. flags in our honor. From the proceeds of the calendar sales, Pin-Ups For Vets has purchased thousands of dollars of new therapy equipment for VA Hospitals across the U.S., and our Pin-Ups For Vets Ambassadors have personally delivered the calendars at the bedsides of over 12,000 Veteran patients on our 50-State VA Hospital Tour. The Vets often tell us, "When you are here, my pain is gone!"

Not long ago, I received a letter from a Veteran I had visited in a VA Hospital. He wrote, "To go from being a highly regarded Marine Infantryman in combat to a patient on a locked psychiatric ward was one of the most de-humanizing experiences I have ever been through. I was the only Veteran there from the Iraq War. I felt weak, embarrassed, and lonely, but your calendar and your visit made me feel a little bit like a hero again. It was a scary place to be. Thank you so much for that visit and for your calendar gift. You are an amazing person and a Hero, and I will always be grateful for that visit."

In real life, I couldn't be with my grandfather, but through the magic of modern photo editing and "through all kinds of weather", here is grandfather and granddaughter, and as the song says, "Just a-traveling along, singing a song, side by side."

Pin-Ups For Vets
501c3 Non-Profit Organization
www.pinupsforvets.com/
www.facebook.com/pinupsforvets
twitter.com/pinupsforvets

GUIDO VAN DE WIEL

How my dad brought life to the community, risked his life as a spontaneous First Responder and gave his life to cancer.

Must one be a firefighter, a marine, or a trauma-doctor to be a First Responder? Or could a teacher, a tutor, a dean, an elderman, a board member of a family care foundation, a chairman of the local harmony orchestra also be seen as a First Responder too? My father was all this. And more.

For a big part of his life, my dad could be seen as a community-based and municipal First Responder. Many times he was the first to intervene on social injustice and took every chance to build the local community.
As a teacher, tutor, and dean, he intervened very early when he saw that new child at his school have a severe setback in terms of language development. And when he started as chairman of the fanfare, he saw a burning platform: at his arrival, the fanfare was an incrowd union where the average age was 55. The last time they welcomed a new member was already 15 years ago. My father transformed this fanfare that had their rehearsal in the pub into a blossoming harmony orchestra that rehearsed in the community house. After the transformation there was a main orchestra, which became concours winners several times, there were two youth orchestra's, different music teachers for all the instruments, lots of new instruments bought by the club, more sponsors than ever, committees for instrument maintenance, et cetera. He had won over eighty new members, one by one; sipping coffee at many kitchen tables. When my father was severely ill, five years later, the harmony orchestra showed honor to him by bringing a serenade at our house where he lay in bed looking through the windows. He answered the orchestra with a slow but determined hand rising, ending in a thumbs up. During his funeral in 1996 the harmony orchestra paid tribute once more to him by playing the music peace Concerto d'Amore that my dad had bought in better physical conditions himself as a music score for the orchestra. A few months before he died, he got proclaimed a royal Knight in the Order of Oranje-Nassau for all his community work and leadership roles he had taken: from board member of the family care foundation to his role as elderman. His pioneering activities in different committees and groups were always boosting the local

community. Yeah, he was a First Responder to the community and brought life to it.

Once my dad became a First Responder in an emergency situation. It was at the beginning of the eighties when we stayed with our caravan in Austria at a campsite. The camping was quite sloping. While we were having lunch in our open caravan porch, new tourists, a married couple, arrived. They were looking for a spot to park their caravan. From the kind lady at the reception, they obviously got different options that were all suitable places for their caravan. We could see from under our open porch how the woman was checking different spots. Then she found a place that she apparently liked, near the top of the hill. The man drove slowly uphill. About 50 meters away from our own camp location, the man started to ungear their caravan. He detached the coupling head from the tow ball of the car and winded the jockey wheel down. He parked the car next to their chosen spot.

Then the couple got in a verbal fight. What the provocation was, was not clear for us from such a distance, but at one moment, the woman was exclaiming and yelling to her man. Then the woman tried to move the caravan by herself. Right after the woman snapped the caravan of the parking brake, she lost herself in another verbal fulmination full of fury towards her husband. While she started her next rant, she turned towards him and the caravan started to roll downhill. At first slowly, then faster and faster. Nor the man neither the woman reacted on the events that were now set in motion. Sitting around our foldable lunch-table we could see in the corner of our eye where the caravan was heading to. There were other caravans standing, a field full of smaller and larger tents, unnoticeable if there were people sitting inside; there were even playing some small children at the bottom of the hill. If nothing was to be done the consequences could be tragical. The caravan was accelerating and it found its way heading towards the lowlands. The small path made of asphalt took a turn, yet the caravan went straight downward. First the upperpart of the caravan hit a branch of a tree, but that did not stop its way down. We were sitting close to the path that the battered caravan now took, yet we found ourselves not in the danger zone.
My father was sitting with his back towards the scene and tried earlier not to pay too much attention to the quarrelling couple. Once he saw what was about to happen, he jumped up from his camping chair, as if stung by a bee. He didn't hesitate and ran towards this white and monstrous trailer-vehicle that was only seconds away from playing a starring role in this catastrophe.

In an agile way he jumped towards the jockey wheel and its handbrake, for which he had to proceed the frontside that had developed already quite some speed. He only had a fraction of a second to pull the brake. He needed to be "first time right", otherwise he would be caught under the weight and the wheels of this white and thunderous cargo. Was it still stoppable or had it gained already too much velocity? He got one chance. If he wouldn't be able to pull the handbrake fast and firmly enough, the caravan with its steel shaft and drawbar would topple him and he would have been ran over by hundreds of kilograms ...

He managed to pull the break in one swift move and stayed unharmed himself. Not a scratch. Because of his action the caravan of this arguing couple came to a halt. And life continued.

Life continued until the day my father heard he had cancer. Then life stopped for a moment. Concerning his disease, he didn't ask: 'why me?' Instead he asked himself the question: 'why not me?' He stayed humble and grateful for everything that life had brought him. He became a First Responder regarding a new medical treatment that was still in the experimental phase. The core of this treatment was that he had to lie down in a big tube, where his body temperature was risen to a condition of artificial fever. Even during this treatment in this ultra-sauna environment, he reacted with a slow but determined hand rising, ending in a thumbs up.

My father had three brothers and three sisters. From all seven, he was the First Responder to God.

Before my dad stopped the caravan he was already my hero. When he showed me how to handle an incurable disease he became my super hero. He always was, have been and will be. He taught me how to live, learned me in what cases I should risk my life, showed me how – and hopefully learned me how – to die, once that day has come. I hope I will respond just like my father. ∎

Guido van de Wiel (Wheel Productions) is a Dutch (ghost) writer, executive coach at two business schools and is awarded Trendwatcher of The Year 15-16. His most favorite team consists of four people: his wife Else, himself and their two kids, Sterre and Bram. His theme for 2018 is Coddywomple. http://www.wheelproductions.nl

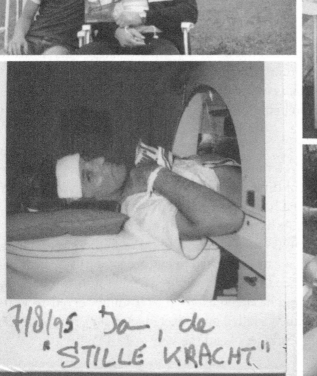

7/8/95 Jan, de
"STILLE KRACHT"

HENRI SUISSA

HERO: *"a man of pristine courage, integrity and honor; relentless pursuit of excellence that places his Nation close to his heart"*-Dr. Suissa

A southern boy that grew up to be an American Hero
The story of CSM, USA Thomas Williams, MPA
US Army Retired Ranger

Unfortunately, our paths never crossed in the United States Army; however, there is an unbreakable bond that Veterans share, and I am the fortunate one to have Thomas Williams in my life. What I would have done to have deployed with Tommy! No better or well-trained human being to have your "back"!

As most combat disabled Veterans, we cohabitated in the same parts of the world, at much different times. We share stories and I marvel with the utmost respect at a man that has always placed the United States Army before anything in his life. As a former Law Enforcement Officer and member of a Special Weapons and Tactics Team (SWAT) there is a shared and mutual respect for what each of us had to endure in our lives. I can say with full faith and confidence that what I witnessed pales into comparison as to what Tommy has seen and has been exposed to. Tommy served 16 years in one of the most highly trained, skilled and coveted special operation forces in the World. Their motto "Rangers Lead the Way"—RLTW!!

Tommy is a man of God, with the utmost faith in the Lord and loves his family with all his heart.

Tommy is very blessed as he is married to the love of his life, a Soldier, SFC Candice D. Williams formerly of Las Cruces, NM. They have two beautiful daughters, Karina and Karolina. Outstanding, well behaved, scholastic and athletic teenagers.

Tommy officially retired from the United States Army on February 1st, 2018 after serving our country for over 22 years. Not only to rise to the ranks of a Command Sergeant Major (CSM), but to do so in such a pace is unprecedented. To achieve the highest and most respected rank of a

Non-Commissioned Officer in the US Army is unconscionable. To do so as a Ranger and in a short amount of time is to be commended and revered. Conversely, there are not too many Military Members that display his moral courage, attention to detail, love and compassion for his Soldiers and fellow man! Tommy will say otherwise, as he is a very humble person and will always down play his accomplishments. I am here to refute this and say unequivocally if he would have continued to serve he would have made CSM of the entire Army! He is that special of a man! However, he retired because being a great father and fantastic husband is highly valued and he states, "Sir, I already missed so many memories". I often talk with Tommy and state "Tommy, your family loves you unconditionally and so does the United States Army". He is a "Hero" and he deserves everything good that he has coming to both him and his loving family!

Tommy was born and raised in Pulaski, TN. *If you ever come across a person from Pulaski, TN you will never "mistake there laid back way of communicating"! As a matter of fact, I often find myself communicating with a nice southern draw!!!* Tommy has an older brother, Mr. Harold Williams that is his best friend. There is a mutual admiration between the two. *Tommy often refers to Harold as "my Hero"!!* Tommy and Harold's relationship is extremely rare. Two brothers that have unconditional love for each other.

They both are soft spoken, fierce competitors with an unmatched work ethic. They are prideful, dedicated and display trust and integrity that gives you supreme confidence in everything they do!! Tommy frequently thanks Harold for being the rock that allowed him to "deploy 13 times to combat". Harold and the love of his life, Janet, are very close to SFC Candice Williams. Concurrently, SFC Williams is the epitome of one of the strongest people I have ever met. Her strength, dedication and support to her husband is unmistakable. Her will and desire to serve this great Nation parallels Tommy. Candice recently completed an executive MBA. While Tommy deployed as an Army Ranger with the 1/75th Ranger Battalion a total of 13 times, Candice was responsible for taking care of their precious daughters and moving their house hold goods all over the globe. As a Soldier, we know that we are only as effective as our "household". For instance, when I deployed, my beautiful spouse Stephanie, advised me "honey, come home safely and I got your 6". Not only did Candice continue to manage the home front, she kept it stable and was both "mom" and "dad"; all while she continued to serve her Nation with the highest esteem. This is truly and American family, with the highest form of character and love for our Nation.

Tommy enlisted in the United States Army, June 1995 and attended Basic Training and Infantry Advanced Individual Training at Fort Benning, Georgia. He will tell you, "Sir, I enlisted as I needed money for College". What appeared to be a very short stay in the Army, turned into a decorated combat disabled Veteran who retired as a Command Sergeant Major (CSM) and member of one of the most highly touted special forces in the Universe; 1st Battalion, 75th Ranger Regiment.

Tommy frequently refers to his father as a disciplinarian that taught him the values of hard work, honesty, strong character, and to never settle for mediocrity. Tommy's father always stated "son, be sure to keep the family together always". According to Tommy, his father was the "glue" to the family". Tommy's parents instilled tremendous values and were outstanding parents and role models. Tommy and I often share stories of both our mothers, and they were both cut from the same cloth. Tommy's mother made him promise that he would complete his Master's Degree and to ultimately complete his Doctorate. Ironically enough, I completed my Doctorate Degree as a promise that I made to my late mother! There is no doubt in my mind, that Tommy will one day be called Dr. Williams!

Tommy is by no means a large man in stature; approximately 5'10 and a 190 lbs. Although retired from the Army he keeps himself in remarkable shape. I made the mistake of challenging him in the gym; fair to say I was on the wrong side of that challenge"!!! Harold will tell you that in high school "the boy was small, but he would hit you in the mouth, he was scrappy". Harold often talks of how Tommy played Varsity Football and that "he would not back down". Both the boys would hunt together and grew an unbreakable bond that would eventually reunite both of their families. Moreover, although we are all quick to judge individuals based on first impressions, Tommy's heart is unmeasurable and there is nothing that he cannot accomplish, nor defeat. He is a winner and a champion!

Tommy served in high visibility and profile positions and retired a decorated Soldier. His previous positions and duty assignments include: Squad Automatic Riflemen, M240; Machine Gun Team Leader; Rifle Fire Team Leader; Rifle Squad Leader; Rifle Platoon Sergeant while serving with C

Company, 1st Battalion, 75th Ranger Regiment. Moreover, reconnaissance/ Sniper Platoon Sergeant and Assistant Operations NCO, HHC, 1st Battalion, 75th Ranger Regiment; Rifle Company First Sergeant, B Company, 1st Battalion, 75th Ranger Regiment, Hunter Army Airfield, GA.

Additionally, Tommy's career path continued with the following duties: HHC/Ranger Selection and Training Company, RSTB, 75th Ranger Regiment, Fort Benning, GA; Division G3 Training SGM, 1st Infantry Division; Battalion Command Sergeant Major, 2nd Battalion, 16th Infantry Regiment, 4th Infantry Brigade Combat Team, 1ST Infantry Division, Fort Riley, KS. CSM Williams' final assignment was the United States Army Sergeants Major Academy, Fort Bliss, TX where he served as the **Dean of Professional Military Studies and Executive Director of Staff and Faculty.**

He has deployed in direct support of both **Operation Enduring Freedom and Operation Iraqi Freedom (13) times as a member of a Joint Special Operations Task Force.** His positions held during combat operations include: **Assault Force Leader, Ground Force Commander, Joint Task Force (JTF) Liaison and JTF SGM.**

Tommy deployed with Task Force 2-16 to East Africa as a member of Combined Joint Task Force Horn of Africa in direct support of Operation Enduring Freedom – Horn of Africa where he served as TF 2-16 CSM and **the Senior Enlisted Leader for all Army personnel.** Tommy's military schooling includes Commandants Pre-Command Course, Brigade and Battalion Pre-Command/CSM Courses, Command Sergeant Major Development Program, all NCOPDS courses, including the United States Army Sergeants Major Course (Class 62), Army Force Management Course, Command Sergeants Major Legal Orientation Course, United States Army Ranger School, Airborne School, Pathfinder School, **Jumpmaster School, Survival Evasion Resistance and Escape (SERE) Level C; and SERE 245.**

Additionally, he has completed Explosive Entry for Rangers Breaching Courses (Basic/Advanced), Dynamic Entry Breaching Course, Assault Climbers Basic Course, Barnhart Advanced Shooting Course; Rifles Only Long-Range Shooting Course, French Desert Commando Course, Combat Lifesaver Course, Ranger First Responder Course, Tactical Combat Casualty Care Course, Senior Training and Education Managers Course and Faculty Development Program, Phase 1 & 2 Courses.

CSM Williams' civilian education includes a Bachelor's Degree in Social Science from Upper Iowa University, a Master's Graduate Certificate in Project Management from Villanova University, and a Master's Degree in Public Administration from the University of Texas at El Paso.

CSM Williams' awards and decorations include: **Legion of Merit, Bronze Star Medal (2)**, Defense Meritorious Service Medal, Meritorious Service Medal (4), Joint Service Commendation Medal, Army Commendation Medal (5), Joint Service Achievement Medal (2), Army Achievement Medal (4), Valorous Unit Award, Joint Meritorious Unit Award, Good Conduct Medal (7), National Defense Service Medal (2), Global War on Terrorism Expeditionary Medal (2), Global War on Terrorism Service Medal, Afghanistan Campaign Medal (3), Iraq Campaign Medal (5), Non-Commissioned Officers Professional Development Ribbon (5), Army Service Ribbon, NATO Service Medal (Iraq/Afghanistan/Sudan) and the Overseas Service Ribbon (3). He has also been awarded the Combat Infantryman Badge, Expert Infantryman Badge, **Ranger Tab**, Master Parachutist Badge, Pathfinder Badge, Army Physical Fitness Badge, and multiple foreign decorations including German, South Korean, and South African Parachutist Badges and the French Desert Commando Badge.

CSM Williams is also the recipient of the National Infantry Association Order of Saint Maurice: Legionnaire Award and the United States Field Artillery Association Order of Saint Barbara.

CSM Williams' civilian affiliations include: Centurion Military Alliance Board of Directors, Fort Worth Chamber of Commerce, University of Texas at El Paso (UTEP) Alumni Association, UTEP Public Administration's Board of Advisors, Upper Iowa University Alumni Association, Project Management Institute, Student Affairs Administrators in Higher Education (formerly known as NASPA), Phi Alpha Honor Society, Association of the United States Army, United States Army Sergeants Major Association, **National Infantry Association**, United States Field Artillery Association, 75th Ranger Regiment Association, 1st Infantry Division Association, Armed Services YMCA, Veterans of Foreign Wars and the American Legion.

When you go through and research what these medals, ribbons and accolades stand for, you become shocked and dismayed. I encourage anyone who reads this story to please look these Medals up and read their history.

I still recall the day that I met Tommy. Candice and United Veterans Construction and Landscape Solutions, Inc. does business with her company; Full Disclosure Background Screening, LLC. Candice stated "Sir, my husband will soon be retiring, and he wants to work with Veterans and I would love for you to meet him". Tommy was in town and he stopped by our office. From the second I met Tommy I was graced by a person of the highest character, professionalism, and respect. We chatted for a while and I then walked him around our organization. I explained to him our Vison and that we were a Veteran Centered organization. He explained to me that he was looking for a fellowship and then work after retiring. As we approached our office I said, "What do I have to do to offer you a fellowship". Concurrently, "when you are done with your fellow ship you have a job". I knew when I was presented with a rare talent and a man of honor. Tommy depicted everything I wanted this organization to stand for.

This story is about a young American boy that was raised with outstanding values, ethics, and integrity. What started out as a mission to seek funding for College turned into a tale about an "American Hero". A boy from a small southern town that worked with an "intensity unknown to mankind"! A passion and a thirst for knowledge that was and is beyond reproach. A man that developed into a leader, mentor, and emblem of the greatest fighting force in the World. Highly educated, compassionate, a warrior mindset, a victor, a champion, and a "Hero"!

Tommy leads by his actions and his ability to conceptualize information is off the charts. He is my Director of Business Development; served as the Interim Operations Director and help stabilize and significantly improve both Departments. Harold is now our Operations Director and his beautiful and loving spouse is our Office Manager. An American family that has sacrificed more for this Nation than anyone I know. Just as Candice has always been his "love of his life, his confidant and security", but for her introduction of him to me, this never happens. Candice Williams, you and Tommy are destined to continue and change lives and provide Veterans opportunities they earned. Tommy you are a man that I admire, cherish our friendship, and you are one of my "Heroes"!!! By the way Tommy, you honored your fathers' wish "by keeping the family together"!! May God continue to bless you, your beautiful family and this great Nation---HOOAH! #TEAMOFTEAMS---Dr. Henri Suissa

HOLLY MAGNAN

A DADDY IS A DAUGHTER'S FIRST LOVE
A TRIBUTE TO Kenneth Montgomery
NAVY, FBI, ATTORNEY, CHRISTIAN, DADDY

There are many words that can be used to describe Kenneth Montgomery. Ken was loving, kind, generous, intelligent, an agent, an attorney, an advocate, a business man, a servant, a Veteran, and a Christian. Ken was a man of great character. He was loyal, honorable and a true gentleman. He had a wonderful sense of humor and had the ability to make everyone in the room feel welcomed and comfortable. You may ask how I know this to be so. Well, I had the profound privilege and honor of being his daughter.

Since my father was a humble man he would probably describe himself as an ordinary, hard working man who just tried to do the right thing and to do his personal best in life. As someone who was able to watch him walk through this life, I would describe him as extraordinary and exceptional. He was my hero!

My father taught me through his actions as well as through his words. He showed me the importance of honoring your elders by the way he honored his Grandpa Boyer. My dad loved his grandpa and valued his opinions greatly and respected him immensely. In fact, he always brought him along on his first date with a girl. The three of them would go to a cowboy movie of Grandpa Boyer's choice. One can only imagine what my dad's date would think about this. According to my dad, if a date was not okay with Grandpa Boyer coming along, then the date just didn't happen. My dad was loyal to his grandpa. He respected Grandpa Boyers opinion. He wanted him to know he was valued and loved. At the end of the evening, Grandpa Boyer would give the girl thumbs up or thumbs down. When my dad told his first date stories, I could always feel the love, the loyalty, and the respect he bestowed upon his grandpa. My dad even instilled a love of cowboy movies in my daughters. To this day, when a John Wayne movie is on we all smile and remember my dad.

After graduating from high school, my dad enlisted in the U.S. Navy. He was stationed in Guadalcanal where he served as an aerial photographer in the VD-1 Squadron during WWII. The mission of this squadron was to photograph and gather intelligence used for the mapping of large areas of enemy held territories. It has been reliably estimated that (during WWII) up to 90% of all tactical military intelligence about the enemy came from photographic sources. In fact, all four Navy Photo Squadrons operating in the Pacific (VD-1, VD-3, VD-4, and VD-5) were awarded the Navy Unit Commendation. Never once did I hear my dad speak in a braggadocios way regarding his service. On the contrary, he spoke with high regard for the other men who served in his unit. He told me he had scary moments during his time in the Navy. He always made others large and himself small, when in reality, his job was extremely dangerous. He, along with a pilot and a gunner, flew into uncharted enemy territory. My father showed me what it means to serve others, to put yourself last, and to care for those who are in need. In my eyes, that is the definition of a hero.

Upon returning home my dad knew he wanted a career that would help others. He decided to go to college and law school, but his family did not have the money for him to attend college, much less law school. The reality was that his family needed him to provide an income. Although he was able to use funds from the G.I. BILL towards his schooling, he was still short the money he needed to make it work. This is when my dad showed what he meant by "always keep your priorities in order." His priority was to graduate and go on to advocate for those who needed help within his community. He kept his "priority" at the front of his mind while he worked three jobs while going to law school. He worked at an all-night fruit stand, he dug graves at a local cemetery, and he and a law school buddy had a "house washing" service. My dad never whined about not having the complete funds necessary for school. He never expected someone else to pay his way in this life. Instead, he went out and worked for the funds to pay for his own schooling and take care of his family. He taught me the importance of hard work and "doing a job right." He made it very clear that doing your personal best mattered. I have tried to pass this on to my daughters as well. I want them to know this is where real self esteem comes from. They also know this wisdom comes from their Pop Pop whom they adored. While at Stetson University Law School my dad was Treasurer of Phi Alpha Delta; Vice-President of the Senior Class; and a member of the Chapman Law Club. My dad had a professor, Dr. Curtis, who he considered a mentor. One of his proudest moments was when Dr. Curtis presented him with Black's Law Dictionary for making the top score in his class. That dictionary sits in my office as a reminder for me to do my personal best.

Immediately after graduation my dad was recruited into the Federal Bureau of Investigation. At this time the Director of the FBI was J. Edgar Hoover. My dad was involved in the SOLO Double Agent Program and a number of other Federal matters. He told stories of he and his partner Harry. For a time, they worked on bank robbery cases. He said they always had each other's backs and took care of each other when they were in a dangerous situation. A photo and a note to my dad from Director Hoover hangs in my office. My dad eventually left the Bureau to go into private practice as an attorney. Although he cherished his days as an agent, he always wanted to serve in a closer, more personal way. He had a passion to be "producing and contributing" as he liked to call it.

In the early 1960's my dad met the late U.S. Representative C.W. Bill Young and the late U.S. Representative William (Bill) Cramer. They all became fast friends and remained good friends throughout their lives. My dad worked with them during the years of the political ICY Machine (Insco, Cramer, Young) of Pinellas County. In the late 60's my dad worked with Congressman Young while he was the Minority Leader of the Florida State Senate. Dad was the attorney for the Legislative Delegation. My dad's legal career also included being a City Prosecutor, an Assistant State Attorney, and the private practice of law. He was a member of the St. Petersburg Bar Association, the Hillsborough County Bar Association, and was a 50-year member of The Florida Bar. One would think those would have been my dad's most accomplished and proudest moments of his legal career, yet, they were not. Those moments came later when my dad practiced Eminent Domain in Hillsborough County. My father felt a true connection with so many of his clients. He felt their heartache as they were being displaced from a generational family home by a governmental authority for a public purpose without their consent. My dad, along with my mom, who was his office manager, made it their mission to protect and serve them. To be their advocate! Many of my dad's clients would stop by the office with guava pastries, black beans and yellow rice lunches, and baskets of backyard fruit. This meant more than any amount of money could mean to my parents. The thank you notes, the hugs of gratitude, the birthday cards, and the homemade treats are what gave my dad meaning in his practice of law. I watched both of my parents listen with respect and care to my dad's clients. I saw them work extremely long hours. They did so happily. From this, I learned the true meaning of life. We are put on this planet to impact each other's lives in a positive way.

The most important thing I learned from my dad is what true, everlasting, unwavering love is. My dad gave it to all of us. He gave it when he served his country, when he was an advocate for those in need, when he honored his family and friends, and when he extended a helping hand to someone he just met. But, most of all he gave it to my mother. He always called her "his sweetheart." I can recall hearing my dad recite poetry to my mom in the mornings. He sang "Let me call you sweetheart" to her all the time. He was a gentleman that treated my mom like a lady. Some may say this "old school" behavior has come and passed. My dad would disagree. He taught me that a man is loyal, honest, and trustworthy, and that "actions speak louder than words." My parents were madly in love with each other and were best friends as well. They worked together in his law practice and were partners in every sense of the word. I am extremely thankful I had them as role models.

My dad passed away August 23, 2015. Not a day has gone by that I have not missed him dearly. Somehow the world was safer, brighter, and more colorful with him in it. He gave a warmth to this planet. He was an uplifter, a giver, and an honorable man. He contributed to the well-being of those in his community, his friends, and his family. He truly cared about everyone! In fact, he never met a stranger. He found delight in socializing with all people and loved learning about their passions, goals, and interests. My dad always had a smile to offer, an ear to listen, a word or two of encouragement, a piece of wisdom to share (the kind of wisdom that comes from experience and insight), and a heart to love. I once heard a phrase that has resonated with me. "A daddy is a daughter's first love." How true this phrase rings for me. Not only was my father my first love, but he taught me how to love and be loved. My dad has now left this world for a better place. But, I am grateful that God will reunite us one day. I know I am saved and will see my sweet father once again. I am so grateful for God's blessing of a beautiful life. I am thankful for everything the Lord has given me and each night I tell Him so. But most of all, I am thankful that He chose Kenneth Montgomery to be my daddy, and my first love.

JASON JOHNSON

K-9 Flash
Yakima Police Department Narcotics Detection K-9 from 2005-2013
Project K-9 Hero Ambassador 2016 – Present
By Jason K. Johnson - Handler/Trainer/Owner

I would like to pay tribute to K-9 Flash who was my K-9 partner at the Yakima Police Department from 2005-2008. I was selected to participate in a narcotics detection course at the Washington State Patrol in the fall of 2005. Prior to that class, we were selecting dogs that possessed certain drives to train from start to finish. As we were testing for dogs in local humane societies and animal shelters, we came across Flash who was picked up on the streets of Everett, WA. Flash was only nine months old and had no home, no name, and no family. Because of her troubled background of living on the streets, Flash had an animal aggression issue that was going to make her unadoptable into another home. She was scheduled to be put down just one day before we decided to take her in for Police K-9 training.

Once Flash got in the narcotics detection program she excelled during her second chance at life and was the only K-9 in her class to score 100% on her certification. Flash went on to serve at the Yakima Police Department until 2013, and even remained in service when I left the department to go work as a K-9 Handler for the U.S. Ambassador in Iraq and Afghanistan. Flash retired in 2013, after totaling up 3000 deployments and over 2200 narcotic related K-9 finds. Since I was Flash's initial handler, I got the opportunity to retire her with me full time and to have her come live with me even though I had since moved out of Washington State and was working in the D.C. area training explosive detection K-9's for the federal government.

After I had trained nearly 2000 dogs around the world for local, state, federal and International Police agencies, I noticed that these heroes were not properly being taken care of retirement. What most people don't know is that when K-9 Heroes like Flash retire all funding is cut for their medical costs, surgeries, medication, food, and death benefit assistance. Looking at my retired hero Flash, and all that she had done for her community, I was inspired to form the Project K-9 Hero Foundation and have K-9 Flash as our Ambassador.

In 2016, Flash and I started the foundation and began taking in retired K-9 Heroes like her who have special needs or are a financial burden on their owners. The Project K-9 Hero Foundation has now taken care of dozens of retired K-9 Heroes from all over the nation who honorable and faithfully served their country. Our goal is to make sure no Police K-9 or Military Working Dog Hero ever has to go without medical care just because funds are not available to them. We provide up to $3000 a year in medical care, food, and death benefit assistance to each hero admitted into our program.

To give back and say thank you to communities all across America, Flash has her own children's book called, "K-9 Flash Becomes a Hero". At the age of 14, Flash still travels the nation and we read her true life's story to children at schools spreading awareness for the needs of retired K-9 Heroes like her and inspiring children about the profession of being a Police or Military K-9 Handler.

Flash also has her very own children's shirt that is made by Nine Line Apparel and in 2018 was nominated as the American Humane Hero Dog Awards Law Enforcement Dog of the Year. Flash has inspired many people along her journey but most of all Flash has inspired me. Flash has taught me that no matter what odds may be stacked against you, it is possible to overcome anything in life. After all, Flash was only one day away from euthanasia before she got her chance to become a Police K-9, and then when given the opportunity she shined like no other.

I have a quote that I use when I speak to large groups of children or professionals about Flash and her story. "Save a dog's life, and they will change yours forever", which is my own quote and it rings so true every day. I have now dedicated my life to caring for retired Police K-9 Heroes like Flash because she taught me that heroes like her deserve better than what we are giving them.

To thank Flash, I volunteer hours of time seven days a week as the Founder and CEO of the Project K-9 Hero Foundation. I ensure that law makers understand that we have no programs or funds in place to take care of our K-9 Heroes medical costs in retirement. Not only will I ensure Flash receives the best possible care in her retirement, I will ensure that hundreds of other K-9 Heroes like her are also afforded the same benefits under the donations we take in to the Project K-9 Hero Foundation and those we serve under its name. Thank you Flash for inspiring me to make the world a better place, but if I could ask her just one question it would be, "who saved who?'

Jason K. Johnson
Founder of Project K-9 Hero
www.projectk9hero.org

Jennifer Brauch

Deputy Donald J. Brauch, Sr
Deputy Sheriff Patrolman, K-9
DuPage County Sheriff, Wheaton , IL
Serviced - Sept 1991 to Friday, August 18, 2006

I am entering a phase of my life as a wife where I have been thrust into a caregiver role, not by choice, but because of destiny. My husband was a K-9 handler, Master K-9 Trainer for many years. He has a plethora of specialties to include, gang officer, juvenile officer, Sniper, Deputy Patrolman, baseball coach, HVAC-R Tech, Master Certified Mechanic, carpenter, electrician, plumber, remodeler, and handicap accessible platforms. Don has always had the gift and calming influence in high risk dispatched calls that he was assigned to while in patrol. He has a gift for thinking outside the box. The numerous calls that he has had over the course of his career span the scale of minute to very serious homicide calls. The final call was the most serious of his career, unbeknownst to him would be his last call to duty.

Don was assigned a call for a possible terrorist threat at a local airport. While he and another Deputy Patrolman were responding, he was broadsided at an intersection by a driver on a cell phone at @ 45-50 mph, causing his squad car to be bounced off the curb and struck twice. Don suffered many permanent injuries to his body. The most serious one being a Traumatic Brain Injury, ending his career that day.
Most of the specialists believe at some point, he lost consciousness after the accident. Even though he was injured, he managed to force open his mangled door that was pinched at the firewall causing injury to his shoulder. He knew even injured, he had to check the driver of the offending vehicle for injuries that he may have suffered. Upon doing, so he started to collapse at the scene. His supervisor arrived just in time to place him in the squad car prior to losing consciousness.

Don has always attempted to maintain a positive attitude, but at times, has been frustrated by the lack of education there has been on Traumatic Brain Injury. He has adapted and overcome quite a few obstacles to date, however, the damage has removed all short term memory yet he manages to overcome and function day to day with limits. He never ceases to amaze me and doesn't complain much about what has happened, only the frustration he has for not doing what he loved to do. He has managed to keep his sense of humor where the average person would have given up so long ago. Don has handled plenty of serious calls and yet remains a constant mentor and thinks of others more than himself. He is in every sense of the word a "HERO". He, within the scope of his own pain, pushes through to help anyone and everyone that calls upon what he is capable of providing if possible. After so many years to date, its 12.5 yrs., he continues to make the best of what hands he was dealt.

Don has persevered every trial presented to him. He's fought the good fight and yet remains strong in his Christian faith of God. His faith has provided the platform for him to reach out to others. He has used that faith to help other officers, deputies, firefighters, and emergency responders with questions about how to push and pay it forward in living a rewarding life.

There are never any moments he asks why this happened to him, but attempts to find out how he can use this accident to help others overcome their struggles. Don has since become a foot amputee as well as blind from the fallout of injuries sustained that day in the accident. I dedicate this tribute to a man, who thru his own adversity, remains a constant blessing to his family, friends, and mentors those who call upon him for assistance always.

Jennifer Brauch
(Spouse)

Jennifer Siller-Lasry

Grandpa's Girl: A Tribute to Eileen Doyon and my sons and niece...

Introduction:

Before I begin to share my story, I would like to dedicate this story to my (very own) niece along with my (very own) sons. Since the title is "Grandpa's Girl" originally, I also dedicate this story to Mrs. Eileen Doyon, for encouraging me to share my story through my (very own) heart as a Proud Granddaughter...

This may or may not be the time and place to share this opinion or perspective; however, I strongly believe that my network is truly supportive as an extension of the ideologies and core values that had resonated so well with my late Grandfather. I state this opinion as is, because it is hard to put in words. It is hard to justify, analyze, specify, since it is something beyond words...

I am the proud Granddaughter of a U.S. Army Veteran. There is nothing more important to me than to keep my Late Grandfather's legacy alive. I loved my Grandfather so much! I miss him terribly and it was not until recently, that I had to realize that I have to get back to core values and back to basics!

On this note, I would like to begin with a tribute to Danny Doyon, to Eileen Doyon; and, to All individuals in Our Veteran and First Responder Network, along with everyone who has in some significant way rather, realized how much their loved ones in Service have meant to them and how critical it is for each survived relative, close friend as well as confidant, to share the legacy of loved ones along with respectfully show true sportsmanship to others...

On this note, thank you Mr. and Mrs. Doyon, for I am truly honored to meet two individuals as yourselves, to reference as of what love is of Story Tellers, as Grandpa enjoyed sharing stories as well.

I realize that I just cannot emphasize enough to my sons how vital it is to read books, learn to make due with basic necessities, volunteer, ask questions about what is not understood and how to make a difference in the world where it counts most, whereby doing everyone an incredible Honorable Service by showing Heartfelt Gratitude to Honorable Heroes Worldwide! I also want to emphasize to my sons to join, or rather participate in, programs to educate the youth on career choices that will allow for First Responders to take children of appropriate age groups under their wing. I was so happy to find out where to take Grandpa when he was still alive. It was a pleasure to introduce my late Grandfather to other Veterans, First Responders- and, individuals with similar backgrounds and ideologies that were not to be compromised for anyone or any circumstances!

On this note, I just cannot emphasize enough to my sons how vital it is to read books, learn to make due with basic necessities and volunteer to join or rather participate in programs to educate the youth on career choices that will allow for First Responders to take children of appropriate age groups under their wing. I was so happy to find out where to take Grandpa when he was still alive. It was a pleasure to introduce my late Grandfather to other Veterans, First Responders- and, individuals with similar backgrounds and ideologies that were not to be compromised for anyone or any circumstances!

Although I have to admit that I tend to get teary eyed, it is with Honor, with humility that years had gone by whereby it was difficult to speak up about personal views on aspects of Daily Devotions in which are vital to me personally. Sometimes it takes unforeseen circumstances to overcome obstacles or the fear of letting others down; however, sometimes it takes a heart, a backbone, core values and others with similar core values to allow someone as myself to come forward with a stronger Faith and level of discipline towards personal, professional- and, academic endeavors than ever before shared with anyone. For instance, I have a history of pouring my heart out on paper which has earned me editor's choice awards, recognition with Honorable Mentions, with invitations to contribute to essays, articles and quotes; however, nothing compares to the level of loyalty and gratitude to the Doyons!

In regards to previously contributing my story to Unforgettable Faces and Stories most recent book Starting Over: Stories of New Beginnings, by Author/Mrs. Eileen Doyon, I would like to once again mention Mr. Danny

Doyon. This Gentleman has been not only a devoted husband, not only the best friend and confidant to an incredibly amazing woman with stories of her own to share I am confident to say in this story book as well- in order to reference via social media sites, previously posted/published articles, comments and feedback with a yearning to get more involved in all aspects of reaching out to First Responders and Veterans around the world, I am equally as grateful to each Spouse in the Doyon Household! You two are a great team- as you two Honor Veterans and First Responders from around the Globe!

Back to my Grandparents, I know from referencing my late Veteran Grandfather and my late Grandmother, that being part of Unforgettable Faces and Stories, has enriched my life in more ways than ever before expressed. Thank you Author Eileen Doyon once again, for being the Proud Daughter of a Veteran who had served in the military before both of us were friends. However, I am grateful that I get to spend the rest of my life with you, sharing stories of what our Fathers and Grandfathers would have liked us to share, so that we continue to grow as true friends and help Veterans and First Responders via arts, whether it be through published works and recreational activities along with a friendship that has no limits! You are truly one of my closest friends in the entire Universe, Mrs. Eileen Doyon, so not only are you an Author, for you are as well one of my very own *Pillars of Strength!*

On a final note, I am grateful to everyone in my family and extended family, for taking the time to receive me well to Honor my Veteran Grandpa, *Mr. Herbert Leonard Siller aka Papa Lenny*!

I realize now, Grandpa's family had to survive *The Great Depression*! I need to survive Today's Struggles! I need to get back on my feet somehow and work on earning an income that will provide not only what I need as in the basic necessities, yet as well support the venues, that resonated so well with my late Veteran Grandfather and Veterans and First Responders around the world!

Enclosed are photos of Grandpa and Grandma, myself and Great-Grandchildren…

JOE R JOJO SHELTON

Those who fight Demons/Monsters we all change. It takes you from being a mild mannered person to a person that really doesn't have a lot of Feelings. Officers see way too much crap. Things that we cannot unsee. We all lose our innocence, and most definitely a piece of our humanity.

If an Officer wants to survive, we soon adapt, some not all, of the characteristics. It is necessary to deal with these Demons/Monsters we fight, watch, and arrest. Now with this said, an Officer becomes capable of rage and violence.

There is a difference, however. We keep those monster abilities locked away deep inside ourselves. Our monsters are only let out for the protection of others.

There is a cost for becoming as we do..... They cause us to be damaged goods with SEVERE DEPRESSION, PTSD, SEVERE PANIC ATTACKS, THE LOSS OF OUR FAMILIES DUE TO OUR PROBLEMS, AND EVEN SUICIDE. I know because I have come so close before. Especially near the end of last year.

But keep in mind we are not Demons or Monsters, but these dangerous abilities we carry never do go away. Now the Demons/Monsters That we watch, they get sick pleasures from harming or killing people. The sense of bestowing fear and terror upon the Citizens and Communities from which they are from. They thrive upon this.

Most people honestly do not understand the cost placed upon the good Citizens of our Communities. These would be far greater without us Officers who fight these POS.

So we Officers on the inside and outside, are willing to make that Honorable sacrifice, To Protect and Serve our Communities so that our Communities and Citizens are safe from the Demons/Monsters......

So before anyone judges us, you might want remember this...

We witness and see things that humans aren't meant to see. We have seen horrific things that cannot be unseen. Not once but many of times. We perform the duties of Corrections and Street Law Enforcement. We are all Sworn Officers. We all take the Same Oath, and have the Same Authority. We are Officers of the Law per DCJS and DOJ.... We are the same... We are one.

For we do the job that most people believe are beneath them.

We Officers protect our Citizens and Communities by using the least amount of force necessary. This use of Force is from Show of Force (physical presence), Verbal, Less than Lethal, and up to Lethal. We Sheepdogs run towards the things that people run away from. We will fight any and everything that people fear. Your life is more safe because of us Officers.

The political correctness says that there is nothing worth fighting for.... All people to include us Officers are supposed to be Submissive. This is not the Sheepdogs Way. For we know that there are things worth Fighting and Dying for. And that is keeping our Prisons, Communities, and Citizens Safe from the Demons, Monsters, and Wolves. We Sheepdogs do prefer Peace over all else. But let be known that we have the ability to wage War on the Demons, Monsters, and Wolves. We Sheepdogs believe that fighting what others fear is a Just and Honorable action. To keep Society safe. We Officers are willing to give the Ultimate Sacrifice for our Honorable Belief. Why do we do this? ...... For us Officers, it isn't a choice, it is an Honor to Protect and Serve.

For it is what we are. We are built to do battle against evil.

WE ALL ARE SHEEPDOGS ALWAYS AND FOREVER.

Joe R Jojo Shelton
Disabled Corrections Officer VaDOC #6965

JOSEPH IMPERATRICE

My Tribute to Anthony Imperatrice

In life, there are moments where you are alone, reviewing where you are in life and how you've gotten to that point. You think of the people that have come into and out of your life, some more positive than others, some maybe you wish you never came across at all. There are many people that stand out that have influenced my life in one way or another. To this day my father, Anthony, a retired NYPD Police Officer has been a very big influence in my life. My father entered the New York City Police Department January 9th, 1986. He was assigned to the NSU initiative which focused on the out of control drug and crime epidemic destroying New York City at the time. Shortly thereafter he was assigned to the 17th Precinct patrolling the streets responsible for the United Nations.

My father was always my hardest critic, if I received a B in school, I always had to hear why it wasn't an A. If I had hits during my baseball game it was… "You should be putting the ball over the fence each time". I felt like I couldn't catch a break in life and that my efforts weren't good enough. Looking back, that wasn't his intentions at all. They were to strive for the very best every time and never settle or give up until I achieved exactly that.

My father retired in December of 2001, serving fifteen and a half years due to an injury to his knee which ended his career. My Dad wasn't the person pushing me to be an officer, it was actually quite the opposite. He didn't want me to wear the uniform. He would always say "I want you to be better than me, I want you to have more than what I have someday." Well, what he didn't realize is that I looked up to him. He was my superhero, and it wasn't about being better than him, rather it was trying to be as good as him, the person who influenced me the most as a young boy.

On January 9th, 2006, exactly twenty years to the date of my father's scheduled retirement, I entered the Greatest Police Department in the world, the NYPD. Six months later, upon completion of my training, I was given the greatest gift ever, the exact shield that my father wore on his chest during his time as an officer, Shield #24955. It has been my greatest and most humbling achievement to date. In September of 2011 when I was promoted to Sergeant, giving that "piece of metal" back, although it was a promotion, was the hardest thing I had to do. It was my bond to my Dad. It was something much more that a piece of tin. It was a reason for me to strive for more. Every day I wore that shield, it was a reminder to be the very best I could be, to treat everyone I encountered with respect and dignity, to be a protector over the people that couldn't protect themselves, and above all, to mirror what my father meant to me, a symbol of morals and ethics.

Today, each time I see my father or speak to him, I let him know that I love him, I always thank him, and I talk to him about each of my days. Even now, he is….. My Hero.

By Joseph Imperatrice
BLUE LIVES MATTER-NYC
@Bluelivesnyc-Twitter
Bluelivesmatternyc@gmail.com

JOSH DILLON

Tribute to Scott Dillon

As a little boy, at the age of 4, I began to realize how extra special of a man Scott Dillon was as a person, father, mentor, giver, and first responder. He was not afraid to show when he was struggling with something. He taught us kids to admit when you are wrong by showing integrity by fixing your mistakes and learning from it. By the time I graduated from High School, I knew how to help people in any way that was possible using the selfless ways that he showed us on a daily basis. Scott was always proud of all his children but when it came to my brother, Nick and I, we shared his rough sense of humor. He would always share jokes that he would not say in front of girls, however there was an occasional slip of the tongue, but also taught us how to respect each other and the women in our lives. He encouraged us to learn as much from the world in order to expand our horizons. Scott loved his family and would always be willing to help out wherever he could even if he didn't have the means to help. He showed all of us his passion for God and the church.

Here are some of my favorite memories of Scott that will be passed down in my family for as long as we will remember. I remember that Dad used to take me shooting. He showed us how to respect your arsenal and that weapons are not for messing around. I honestly have more love working with troubled people, having worked security in many fashions, because of Dad's love of helping people. On the plus side this gave me plenty of things to talk about with him that we had in common. I loved being able to talk to Dad and it is one of the things that I miss the most about him. One of my favorite stories is when Dad was driving to get off the expressway in Akron, OH. He saw a homeless woman in a bathrobe on the side of the bypass. Dad pulled the car over, told his family that he needed to do something, and got in the back, then pulled out clothes and a blanket to give her. This is the kind of man that would tell us to not be discouraged by your most vulnerable doubts about yourself and failure. Another story always struck me as being one of Dad's most thrilling police adventures. The day he had his first session of Chemo, later while on duty, he noticed a vehicle that looked suspicious. He remembered a person of interest that had committed a crime and the vehicle matched, he pursued the vehicle and once it stopped the driver tried to make a break for it and Dad tackled him to the ground. When the other officers arrived, they noticed the suspect had soiled himself and one asked, "Did you really have to scare the crap out of him?" Everyone got a good laugh and that story just goes to show how dedicated Scott was to serving the public. One of the most interesting stories was when former President Jimmy Carter was admitted into Metro Health. Dad was assigned protective duty alongside the Secret Service. Jimmy Carter, while making small talk, shared personal interests involving the city of Cleveland and his wonderful view from his window. Dad was a great practical joker. When I was younger and he was still a fire fighter, he loved showing us the fire truck and when we least expected it, he would disappear and pull the horn scaring us into laughter. No matter how many times he did it, he got us every time! Now imagine being around the age of 6 or 7 and being in a large fire house with six garage doors. The other fire fighters were prepared to go at any time; the lights were dimmed waiting for a call to come in. We would be sitting on the front of the truck and just like magic, he would disappear into the darkness. We would try to find him but we could never succeed. The anticipation would build and then suddenly out of nowhere, Dad would blast the horn on one of the fire trucks. We were scared out of our wits while Dad was rolling with laugher in the cab of the fire truck. Dad was a volunteer Fire Fighter at Plain Township Fire and Rescue at Edgefield Station 2 for four years. For about six years, he was part time at the Breckville V.A. fire department in the early 90's. Dad's firefighting career ended when he was the first responder to a chemical hazmat incident that caused vapors to fill the air. The vapors are what caused Dad's different types of cancers to form. He was hospitalized for several months and waited a full year before taking his next steps for a new career. He went to the Police Academy at Akron University and started his commission at Beach City Police department. After a year, he transferred to Metro Health Protective Services. During that time, he was also trying to become a Private Investigator. His dream of being a P.I. came to a halt when he was diagnosed with Lymphoma Non-Hodgkin's disease and needed to begin treatment. While dealing with Chemo, he decided to stay at Metro Health to help the department grow into the well-oiled machine that it is today. Over his fourteen years of remission, Metro Health became a full-fledged Police Department where Scott continued to serve and touch the patient's lives by showing encouragement and sharing his story. He knew the importance of keeping yourself in good mental health while dealing with the bad things that come to us in life. He did his best to keep the patient's spirits up.

For those of you that knew my father or was touched by his kindness, here is his favorite thing to say, "Always remember that there are people who are less fortunate than you. There are people who need help in many ways. And Metro Health can make sure patients and employees receive all the support and care they need." Scott Dillon

Dad's legacy will live on for many generations through all the lives that he touched and the stories that we will share about him. We will also carry on the Dillon Family Tradition of participating in the 4 Leaf Clover, 4 mile run/walk on June 9th in Akron Ohio. All of the proceeds from this race go toward local cancer patients in Northeast Ohio. 2018 is the third annual run. This is the first year Scott Dillon and his wife Deborah participated in the inaugural race. Last year, Deborah ran alone because Scott was too sick. This year the Dillon family is coming out in full force to show our support and respect for this wonderful program. Along with friends, family, and first responders, we are expecting a great turn out. Monica Robins from WKYC Cleveland News, who covered Scott's collection of patches from many branches of first responders all over the world, will be joining us to cover this event and bring recognition to those people willing to help those fighting against cancer. She is helping to raise awareness for the 4 Leaf Clover Race by covering the story on the news and networking to bring more people to participate on race day. My brother, Officer Nick Dillon, and I have been contacting different first responders around the area and in neighboring states to challenge those willing to come out and run in their uniforms. We have both gotten peoples interests and are looking forward to see the turn out.

Josh Dillon
https://runsignup.com/Race/OH/Akron/fourleafcloverrun

JUDITH DILLON

IN MEMORY OF MY SON
SCOTT LOUIS DILLON
1963-2017
UNIONTOWN, OHIO

As a mom, moms are supposed to die before their children, but God had other plans. Scott's legacy will live on in the lives of people who loved him and those who were helped by him. Mom's love never ends. We will meet in heaven someday.

His birth was easy, the doctor said, "You have a fine, baby boy." 6 lb. 12 oz., 21." As he grew, he was always busy, inquisitive and fun loving, running everywhere.

Scott accepted Christ as his personal Savior. I believe that inspired him to have a heart to serve others. He was a young man living in the world but loved Jesus.

His desire to serve others manifested itself as a youngster, age 12…riding his bike to the Uniontown Fire Department and helping his buddy, Chief Kenny Hosey. He was so excited to see what they were doing and help out when he could. He joined the Plain Twp Fire Department then moved on to the Brecksville VA Hospital Fire Department. While at the VA, he was exposed to a dangerous chemical that eventually reared its ugly head as lymphoma. After the VA Fire Department was closed, he joined the University Police Academy and became a policeman. He joined the Cleveland Metro Health Hospital's police team. Eventually lymphoma cancer was diagnosed and treatments began. In recovery, he organized a cancer support group to help others fighting this disease. "Fresh Hope," support group thru Scott, was available to police, firefighters, EMTs just to talk or meet together for support of their cancer issues. Scott had established a police/fire/EMT Patch collection to be auctioned to support various cancer efforts. Please donate Scott's dad, Bob Dillon 13585Amodio Ave. NW, Uniontown, OH 44685.

Working with the police department made Scott ever more mindful for the safety of his fellow co-workers on the force. He was adamant in his effort to procure regular training, better equipment, procedure adherence and safety. He joined the Hazmat team and was part of the Homeland Security team on location. He was also part of the financial giving contributions for the less fortunate people and was recognized for that financial regular giving.

His family, wife and children, came first. He loved his home. He tried to instill honesty, love for others, God, and country, good work ethics and love for each other. He was tough. He wanted each member of family to do their share and be a family team member. He loved his family. His favorite song was Jesus Loves Me, and he sang that to his children.

Because of his previous divorce, he recognized the fact the when mothers get full custody, the fathers get left out of some contacts with children, school involvement, etc. As a result he organized a support group called, "Rights for Fathers Who Care." Later the name changed to "Rights for Parents Who Care" due to women wanting to be a part. This effort took him to the state representative and collaboration with officials to promote shared parenting. His effort was invaluable in establishing help for fathers.

A week before his death, he wanted to be baptized to show his dedication to Jesus and to let his children be influenced by his decision to follow Christ. He didn't make it to the river but was baptized in his bed surrounded by family.   His boys went to the river with the pastor and were baptized. They then went home to tell dad. He squeezed their hand and smiled. Scott died the next day. What a home going!

All that to say this: A legacy of giving of self and helping others was Scott's life. All this through a heart that loved Jesus. Jeremiah 29:11 "For I know the plans I have for you," declared the Lord," plans to prosper you and not to harm you, plans to give you hope and a future.

> Until we meet again,
> I love you son,
>   Your Mom
> (Judith Knotts Dillon)

JULIEANNE WHITE

First Responders are a blessing to all of us regardless of where we live in the World. They are there to protect us, keep us safe, offer compassion and support when needed.

I am very fortunate to have First Responders in my life beginning as a teenager when I was introduced to endurance running by a special unit Detective Sergeant of the OPP (Ontario Provincial Police), Barry Ruhl, now retired. He has written two books of his own life, his struggles and his rewards of serving under the badge to keep all safe. Through our many long runs together and my first marathon at the age of 17 years old, he taught me resilience, determination and courage. He instilled in me fierce independence to never give up despite the challenges you may face along life's journey. He taught me the power of nature, how one can find peace and tranquility with simple happenings in life, to be grateful and appreciative for those who enrich your life and those who have been unkind....there too is a lesson to be learned from their behavior.

My brother, special unit detective OPP, Neil White, who has been a life source of comfort, friendship and love. My older brother with whom I always felt a sense of comfort and security in his presence. He was there to support me through the most difficult days which followed after the death of my husband. He has been there ever since these past 5 and a half years even though we are oceans apart, I know he is always there for me. I have the greatest love for him. We spent our growing years in England together often whether in sport or nature or education, he would encourage me to pursue to the highest level of excellence. If I shall fall short, well then I had at least tried. He would encourage me to never give up because when you are completely worn to the core of your very being, it then grandeur may happen to turn your life around.

My niece, Officer Taylor White of the OPP, I am tremendously proud of her decision to serve as she once thought of becoming a Corporate Lawyer as she maintained a 90-95% average through University whilst playing varsity rugby for her University at Queen's.

My sister-in-law (former) Special Agent Kim Kouri OPP. She has always been supportive of all my endevours as a strong independent woman. She has always offered encouragement when all others doubted my abilities. I have tremendous admiration for Kim not only as an officer, yet a mother, a provider for her family.

Nick & Aloha Peters, Nick, special unit's sergeant \ officer and Aloha, his wife, Sheriff. They have always been there for support and comfort even prior my husband's passing. They have continued their support, friendship and comfort as that of a special family. I honour their dedicated service to the public. I honour their love.

Officers of the Carlsbad Police department for keeping the community of Carlsbad safe. We must never forget all the K-9s who serve proudly to protect for they are officers as well.

Officers of the Sheriff's department and San Diego Police officers, Fire officers, paramedics who keep my family safe. The paramedics who were there for me when my front tire blew out on a downhill section of the road whilst finishing a training ride prior a major International triathlon competition. My jaw was exposed down to bone with a flap of skin hanging, they provided undue compassionate care.

The Fire officers and police officers who safely helped evacuate my horse and myself in the San Diego area of Carlsbad and Elfin several years ago. My friend, Erik Burgan, Fire officer/paramedic who was my run training partner for several years, who helped me capture several course records from half-marathon to marathon to 50km runs. Not only was he there during my athletic career, yet through life changing circumstances beyond my control to offer support and friendship. He, his family and his wife are all very special individuals.

Immense gratitude to all for these past 5 and a half years after the passing of my husband. You have offered to me and my family of animals a special kind of compassion, you have made us feel like family, and you have welcomed me as a British foreign National.

Whilst back in my native England/UK, I have immense amount of admiration and appreciation for all the First Responders here as they have endured some horrific situations of terror attacks. They respond tirelessly despite the demands they face. They are exceptional with their K-9 units and rapid response to dangerous situations as reported in the media. Their stress can be great like all First Responders, and they all deserve more praise from the public at large. One cannot help to be safe in their presence.

God Bless & Heart felt thank you for your dedicated service!
JulieAnne White

KAITLYN ROGERS

Meet Brian Rogers, he is the Chief Operating Officer and a paramedic at Community Ambulance. He began his career in EMS in the Las Vegas valley in 1988 at Mercy Ambulance. But, this is not where his story began, he was a paramedic in New York City starting in 1984, following in his father's footsteps. He credits his father, John, as the reason he began work in this field. Brian's heart for people is what makes him the perfect man for the job. He lives to do right, not only with his patients, but with his employees. He values family which is what he has modeled his work place to be. He believes that it is his job to care for his employees so they can care for their patients. To this day, Brian still loves spending time on an ambulance running calls, because that is the foundation of it all. He is a diligent leader, a passionate paramedic and a loyal man through and through. October 1, 2017 is a night that changed the lives of so many, including Brian. When he was awoken by the call he has feared his whole career, he immediately rushed to the scene of the Route 91 Harvest Festival to ensure the safety of concert goers and his employees. He took charge and did what he does best, save lives. Arriving to the scene, he saw the blood, the tears and fear in people's eyes. He calmed nerves, treated wounds and did the work he would never wish upon anyone. That night he took the unthinkable job of having to pronounce concert goers dead so his employees did not have to walk back into the nightmare they recently lived through. That is just the leader Brian is, not just on that dreadful night but in his day to day life. He truly is a hero in our community.

Meet Brian Rogers, he's my dad. Ever since I was a little girl, he has always instilled love and compassion into my heart not by telling me to do so, but by seeing him do so every day of our lives. Growing up as an "EMS kid", I have seen my father's bravery and tremendous leadership abilities. He has always, and will always, push me to be the best woman I can be. With all of the evil he has witnessed throughout his career, he still helps me see the good in the world and constantly reminds me to focus on the positive aspects of every situation. Not a day goes by where my father does not make sure I am assured that I am loved and cherished. He is the reason I swore my whole life I would never work in EMS, but is the reason I am doing so today. His heart and passion for what he does is something I look up to in so many ways. October 1, 2017 is a night that will forever define the relationship he and I have. No one in this field imagines waking up in the middle of the night to hear that their city is under attack. No father imagines a call coming from their child. My dad clearly remembers the words, "Daddy, they're shooting at me," coming from my mouth under the fear in my voice and tears in my eyes. As he rushed into that scene, he was not only a courageous leader but a father fearing the loss of his child. When he arrived to the scene, after 20 minutes of not hearing from me, I ran into his arms. With a quick I love you and the most calming hug I've ever experienced, he sent me out of the chaos. Though it may not be as extreme each day, he is always my safe place when troubles come my way. He not only shields me from being hurt, but teaches me how to fight on no matter what obstacles come my way. He has taught me how to love so well, be brave and never give up. He is the greatest man in the world, in my eyes. I love him more than I could ever put into words. He's my hero and always will be.

Kaitlyn Rogers

KAT SCHWARTZ

Beyond Resilience

The cool breeze on my skin felt so soothing as the paramedics loaded the gurney into the emergency van. My chest was tight and breathing was difficult. All the muscles in my body felt like they were seizing up. I knew that these gentle men would care for me, as they attentively scanned my body for other symptoms and took time to reassure me that they will do their best to take care of me. While my mind was drifting in and out of a fog, I had no doubts these men would absolutely do their best. And…she was there for me, too.

She thought she had married the man of her dreams, until he quickly began to control every move she made by degrading her every time something did not work out to his favor. She confided in me and I told her that I would be there for her in every sense of being present. Her story was the beginning of long years of an angry man who refused to give up, even after divorce. We cried tears together; I listened (and sometimes put in my two cents worth of advice).

These occurrences, and more, are far in the past now, but reflecting back on them brings sorrow for those times. Yet, there is a rhythm and flow that tends to rise when incidents and accidents occur in my life with my daughter.

She is kind; she puts her life on hold, and shows up when no one else will. My daughter and I are always there for each other, mentally, emotionally, and spiritually. Even though we do not practice the same religion, we practice love. This deep unspoken code of love and commitment seems to connect us.

She showed up on the day I thought my heart was going to stop. Her tender reassuring voice allowed me the shred of strength to keep moving forward with my intent to never give up. She gave me hope.

I tended to her when she was puddled upon the floor in tears and grief as she told me her decision to protect herself and the children and leave him. So many times we embraced each other in plummeting emotions, yet the comfort of knowing someone cared immensely for our wellbeing became the catalyst for our strong futures.

I'd like to say that people of this nature are our First Responders each and every day. Kind hearts that reach out for us when we are in pain. The hand that catches us when we are about to fall.

We rarely hear about these types of First Responders, because we expect this from our sons, daughters, husbands, wives, and society. And, when someone does something with great kindness, in a small gesture, it is noticed. The person who received it, notices. And, this First Responder, just like the ones who are recognized in the media, do not look for glory.

These First Responders are the salt of the earth who have found a deep sense of purpose and wisdom that dwells within each of us.

Our future, as human beings, yearns to see the spirit of the First Responder… not just to rescue or soothe; but, to lay the foundation for every day living. When we live from our hearts, much more is possible and a contented resilience begins to spear through the difficulties of life.

Receiving kindness and care for each other is a birthright that we still need to recognize in all parts of the world. When we help each other heal through trust, confidence, and love, these actions come with ease and humble intentions.

The relationship between my daughter and I is a very special one. We recognize and love our differences because we find ways to give them credence and strength. My intent is not to patronize this relationship, but to bring this story of courage and perseverance to you for your own connection to the yearning for understanding, love, and peace in your life. For it is with only ourselves that we can begin this journey of BEING a First Responder.

Be it in small ways, we can still send a ripple-effect of kindness to others who will feel the same reassurance I felt when the paramedics cared for me, or when my daughter and I reached out to each other and we shared our pain, to be present, and to heal.

Knowing that peace is possible in the throes of chaos allows me to reminisce about the soothing cool breeze that brought me relief in that small moment in time that changed how I felt about the world. So, it is with this message I deliver to you to seek kindness in everything that you do, whether it is being thankful for a drink of water, or seeing the world through curious eyes.

Be grateful for our First Responders everywhere and see them in the smallest of gestures to the most heroic selfless acts of courage. You, too, are a First Responder, if you so choose this path to be kind. For it is when we make this choice, we move beyond the resilience of our mundane lives to creating a world of peace.

By Kat Kohler Schwartz

KELLY PRESTON

Michael Lee Preston was born June 3, 1973. He was the oldest of 3 brothers, who all served in the Marine Corps, along with their father. Mike was a hard worker and started cutting grass to make money at the age of 10. He was a perfectionist from the start. He entered the Marine Corps for 4 years after High School and became a police officer in the winter of 1997.

Mike and I met in 2003 and became fast friends. We had the privilege to work together for 14 years. His sheepish smile and sweet demeanor won my heart over almost instantly. He was 6'3, a huge man but full of love to give. His laugh and smile could light up a room and he never knew a stranger.

Mike had twin girls from a previous marriage and I had a daughter. We soon became a family on October 1, 2015. In 2010 we welcomed our son, and Mike was so excited to have another man in the house. He cried at the ultrasound when they told him that he was having a son.

Mike was always willing to work overtime especially at Christmas to make his children's wishes come true. He enjoyed being a cheer dad and basketball coach for his three daughters. He also helped coach his son's t-ball team. Mike was an accomplished brown belt in Jiu Jitsu. He won the Pam Am in California in 2014, which was a huge accomplishment.

Mike was a hero in every sense of the word. He saved a man's life by providing CPR on the roadside while off-duty when he passed a stopped car on the interstate. He was hailed as a hero again for pulling a handicapped man out of a burning house before the fire department arrived. Mike's life and passion were to serve and protect all he knew.

The last year of his life, he responded to a call where grandparents had been raising their grandkids on a fixed income. Mike saw the struggle and asked the community to donate clothes and toys. It happened to be the same week as Easter so he decided to buy Easter baskets for the 3 children and deliver them Sunday morning.

Mike passed away January 13, 2016. He will be forever missed by all who knew him.

KYLE REYES

They Ask My Why

"You're the CEO of a successful marketing agency. Why would you put it all on the line by throwing yourself in the middle of controversy?"

If I had a dime for every time someone asked me that question, I could have retired years ago.

First – context. My agency is The Silent Partner Marketing. We run the marketing for businesses all across America, producing tens of thousands of videos and spending millions of dollars a year on advertising across digital and traditional platforms.

We're known for lots of things… but the one thing I'm most proud of us our commitment to donating $1 million in services to emergency responders and veterans.

That number started much smaller. But after a video in support of police that we created went viral, we were attacked by internet trolls. We were told we were "racists" and "Nazis" for supporting those who hold The Thin Blue Line. They called for us to be shut down and inundated us with fake 1-star reviews.

So we did what any company filled with patriots should do. We upped the donation and told the trolls to kiss our American asses.

Not long after, I was chosen as the National Spokesperson for Law Enforcement Today. We launched a series called Behind the Uniforms, which takes place at what has become a famous (or perhaps infamous) Whiskey Wall at our studios in Connecticut.

The way the show works is that emergency responders and veterans (along with, in some cases, their supporters) bring a bottle of Whiskey to the wall. We share a drink and they share two stories, telling viewers about a really good day and a really crappy day on the job. The goal is obviously to humanize the men and women "behind the uniforms".

We keep a bottle of whiskey and an empty glass on the bar at all times as a tribute to those who paid the ultimate sacrifice and will never be able to tell their story.

So....why? Why double down on supporting those who hold the thin blue line... when it's resulted in attacks on us, threats of violence and even a loss of some clients?

I could tell you countless stories of my friends who are emergency responders or veterans, and the pain they've endured in service to their country.

I could tell you about my deep pride for my little brother Luke, who (at the time of writing this) is serving our country in Bahrain. I might have gotten the looks in the family, but he clearly got the balls and courage (and arguably the humility... but that's a tossup).

I could tell you about my incredible cousin Danny, who is a police officer on the East Coast and has dealt with some of the most ridiculous crap I've ever heard of.

But it actually stems back to HIS father... my Uncle Dan. Uncle Dan has been a cop for as long as I've known him. Prior to that, he fought in Vietnam.

I'm pretty sure that growing up, every kid had that uncle who sort of scared the shit out of them. That was Uncle Dan. Not because he did anything scary. He wasn't mean. He didn't yell. He was just a ... presence. And I didn't understand him.

Uncle Dan didn't talk much. I think I remember hearing him say about 10 words during my childhood. The main one directed to me or anyone who looked at him: "what?".

Then there were those directed to my cousins: "get in the car" and "ask your mother".

He wasn't a bad guy. He didn't make it to a lot of family functions, because he was often working at the police station. Or – God bless him – he'd figured out a way to avoid the insanity of our family gatherings and at least blame it on work. Either way... I'd say that makes him a pretty good man.

As I got older, I started noticing something. He wasn't avoiding. He was… watching. He was… protecting. I began to understand that my uncle was simply often standing on the sidelines like a watchful giant. He wasn't a big man, but he had a big presence. That fear I had of him turned to a very deep level of respect. I realized that it was part of his DNA to be a Sheepdog.

Last year, two of his kids got married. At the first of the two weddings, my wife and I were enjoying cocktail hour and catching up with family when I scooted off to the restroom for a few seconds. When I walked out… there was my uncle.

"Hey Uncle Dan", I said.

Then… something unexpected happened. A conversation. Like… a long conversation, where he talked about our show Behind the Uniforms and the work we are doing trying to help tell the stories of these men and women who don't get the recognition they deserve.

We talked and talked. And he told me he was proud of me. And appreciated me. And loved me.

My Uncle Day. The man who didn't talk. He. Appreciates. ME.

When I got back to cocktail hour, my wife and my parents asked where I had gone for so long.

"I was with Uncle Dan," I told them.

"What were you talking to him about?" they asked me.

"I wasn't talking to him – he was talking to ME," I told them.

Everyone looked at me like I had two heads. Uncle Dan doesn't talk. He's also not a drinker… so nobody could blame it on bourbon.

Was it possible that *I* had too much bourbon and had made the whole thing up?

No, the impossible had happened. My uncle and I spoke. It felt like I had experienced a rite of passage and, despite the fact that I was married with kids and a successful company, had finally become an adult.

A couple of hours later, my cousin had the first dance. Others joined the couple on the dance floor, all in celebration…sipping, toasting, dancing, singing.

And there was Uncle Dan… standing there with his arms cross on the edge of the dance floor.

Watching. Protecting.

The Sheepdog.

Kyle S. Reyes is the Chief Executive Officer of The Silent Partner Marketing, co-host of The Whiskey Patriots and the National Spokesman for Law Enforcement Today. Reyes is also an acclaimed keynote speaker on patriotism and leadership, entrepreneurship and marketing by storytelling. You can follow him on Facebook.

www.thesilentpartnermarketing.com
www.thewhiskeypatriots.com
www.lawenforcementtoday.com
www.facebook.com/pg/KyleReyesCEO

LARRY CHRISTIAN

In August 2008 our lives were changed forever. It was a hot summer day on a Sunday and I was mowing the yard. I was thinking about how good I felt and how happy I was that my wife and children were healthy. Life was good and my family was abundantly blessed. I noticed that my son, Steven, was sitting on the back patio under the cover. I decided to take a breather and visit with him since I had not seen him in a while. Steven was in college and a scarcity around the house. I saw a worried look on his face as I approached and knew, at that moment, something was amiss. As I sat down next to him I asked what was on his mind. He seemed somewhat embarrassed to tell me what he had to say. Finally, Steven informed me that his testicle was swollen and painful. As we continued to talk, I learned that he has been dealing with this for almost two months as the testicle increased in size. I tried to maintain a poker face and I assured him that everything was going to be ok.

From this point forward, everything was a whirlwind of activity for my wife and me. I quickly made a doctor's appointment for Steven the next morning. The doctor was very concerned and scheduled Steven for an ultrasound. After a couple of days, we met with the urologist for the results of all the tests. As we sat there in his office, I could tell by the look on his face that the news was not good. My son was diagnosed with Stage 3C Embryonal Carcinoma. My son was devastated by the news, as expected from a 21 year old who had his whole life ahead of him.

Steven was a big, burly young man who was tough as nails and hard as a rock. He was an all-district football player in high school and had received scholarship offers from several small colleges. He was the kind of All-American young man that any father would love for a daughter to bring home to meet. He was also very brave and courageous and always stood up for the underdog. I really didn't know the extent of his courage and bravery, but over the course of the next three years I was going to find out.

Steven underwent his first surgery about a week after being diagnosed. After recovering from surgery, he was admitted into the hospital and underwent chemotherapy. I think as my wife and I saw him lying there in that bed, the gravity of the situation started to sink in. The chemo was really knocking him down and made him so sick. I cannot tell you how many times I wept like a baby and cried to God, asking him why he had done this to our family. I was a veteran police officer who was used to being in control of everything about my life and the lives of my family. I could handle any situation and knew everything was going to be okay. For the first time in my adult life, I felt no control.

After Steven completed his chemotherapy, he regained his strength and took control of his situation. He studied about testicular cancer and learned all there was to know about its treatment and prognosis. Steven was a very analytical young man and questioned everything. As he and I were on the road headed to Austin, Texas one morning, he informed me that he had found the doctor to perform his next surgery. He told me that this doctor was world-renowned for this type of surgery in that he can salvage the ability for men to remain fertile and have children. He also informed me that this doctor was in New York City. I knew that my son had researched this and studied it so, we were going to make it happen.

I was employed by the Tyler Police Department in Tyler, Texas and had a very strong group of men and women to help my family and me. When they found out where we were headed for Steven's surgery, they all rallied with support to assist us. A few weeks later, we were on a plane flying to New York.

The surgery in New York was to be laparoscopic and last only two to three hours. It ended up lasting almost twenty hours and the surgeons had to completely open Steven's abdomen to remove supposed "necrotic tissue" which were remnants of the chemotherapy. I forgot to mention, the original cancer had spread to his abdomen from the testis. According to the head surgeon, the necrotic tissue was like glue and had to be painstakingly removed but, unfortunately more cancer was found in this area. Also, the laparoscopic surgery was going to save his ability to have children but that did not work out. After Steven awoke from surgery, we chose to give him the bad news rather than the doctor. He was devastated but his strong will shone through. After two weeks, we left New York to head home. Steven was graciously upgraded to first class and was able to have a comfortable ride home. During the flight, he sent fresh baked cookies back to his mom and dad from the first class section. That was our son, always thinking of others.

About a month later, a different chemo regimen was used to try and kill the rogue cancer cells remaining in his abdomen. We thought the chemo had done its job but we were wrong. The cancer reappeared. I remember the nurse calling me from Steven's oncology office with the bad news. By this time Steven and his twin brother, Matthew, had rented an apartment together. I drove to the apartment to tell Steven, crying all the way while trying to figure out how I was going to break the news to him. Steven took the news hard and punched a hole in the living room wall with his fist. Then, he bravely moved forward.

We learned of a great doctor in Indiana by the name of Lawrence Einhorn. He came highly recommended as he was Lance Armstrong's oncologist during his battle with testicular cancer. A new sense of hope came over us as we made arrangements to head to Indianapolis for "salvage chemotherapy". Dr. Einhorn was a very gracious and personable man. His caring and understanding were impeccable along with his assistant, Jackie. I remember looking in the lobby and seeing the autographed pictures of Armstrong which also gave us much encouragement.

Steven underwent high dose chemotherapy with stem cell transplant. What all that means is, before the chemo started they recovered stem cells from Steven for later use. After receiving each round of chemo, Steven's healthy stem cells were reintroduced into his system so he would not succumb to the high dose chemotherapy. Two long months later the chemo worked and Steven was declared cancer free. I remember how happy Steven and I were as we drove back to Texas. Finally, we were thinking about the future and that included one very special thing that made me exude with pride. Steven and his brother decided they wanted to attend the police academy and follow in their dads footsteps.

It took several months to complete the academy, since both boys had to attend the night classes. One of the proudest days of my life was when they walked on that stage together to receive their respective diplomas. While in the academy, Steven met a young lady by the name of Tchanee. She was a beautiful red-haired girl who had an outgoing personality. She would turn out to be an angel from heaven.

Steven ended up taking the civil service exam for my police department and passed. I remember the day of his physical agility testing. I went to the football stadium where the testing was performed to watch my son. Steven was still recovering from all the chemo he had in the past and was not in the best of shape. He passed everything with flying colors until the 1.5 mile run. It took everything he had in his weakened state to complete that run in the prescribed time frame. I watched a determined young man will himself to not give up. He finished the run with barely seconds to spare. He was so happy and excited as we hugged afterward.

Steven and Tchanee were very much in love by this time and wedding plans were made. My wife even assisted Tchanee in picking out a wedding dress. It was a very wonderful time and we were excited for what the future held for them.

Our joy was short-lived. Steven's cancer came back with a vengeance, but this time in his brain. Over the course of time, it eventually spread to his spinal cord and he became somewhat paralyzed. His bowel function began to shut down and he was unable to swallow. He was taken to MD Anderson in Houston, Texas for a last ditch effort to try and save him. Who was at his bed side? Tchanee. She never left him. Steven knew he did not have much time left on this earth but, he had already purchased a ring for Tchanee. They decided to get married, right there in that hospital room. Their love for one another radiated throughout that hospital. They might as well have been getting married in the Sistine Chapel. Our pastor, David Martin, was at the hospital and he performed the ceremony for them. Steven could barely talk but I believe it was God who gave him the voice to repeat his vows. After the ceremony they kissed to consummate the marriage. There wasn't a dry eye in the house.

We returned home and Steven was placed in Hospice. While in there I gave Tchanee all the authority to make the decisions for her husband. She stayed by his side for the whole duration while watching Steven get weaker and weaker. The commitment and love she showed to our son helped us get through a traumatic time. Also, my patrol partner, Darrell Gardner, was with me 24/7 for two full weeks while at Hospice. He refused to leave my side and, for that, I am forever grateful.

Steven asked his mother to sing the "wake-up" song to him because that was a wonderful memory from childhood. She lay in that bed with Steven and cradled him while singing the lullaby. What a brave woman my wife is. She was devastated but managed to keep her emotions in check. She would wait till she left the room before crying her eyes out. I, on the other hand, broke down in front of Steven. I wept and told him I was not ready to let him go. Steven motioned for me to lay with him in bed. As I lay there, he hugged me and whispered that everything was going to be ok. That gesture from my son meant so much to me and still comforts me to this day.

Steven asked for a piece of paper shortly before he went into a coma. He wrote down a few words as best he could with limited faculties. The note read: "I don't want y'all to be scared of what's gonna happen to me after I die. But I know where I'm going. I never had a doubt. Don't be sad, just know that I will be living with kings and angels. I wish I could say more."

Steven peacefully passed away a few days later in the presence of his family. Steven is our hero and an example of a life well lived. My sadness will always be with me but I look forward to seeing him again, soon. His brother, Matt, is now a patrol sergeant. His sister, Kelli, inspired by her brother received her BSN from UT and is now a registered nurse. Steven's legacy lives on. I love you, son.

Larry Christian

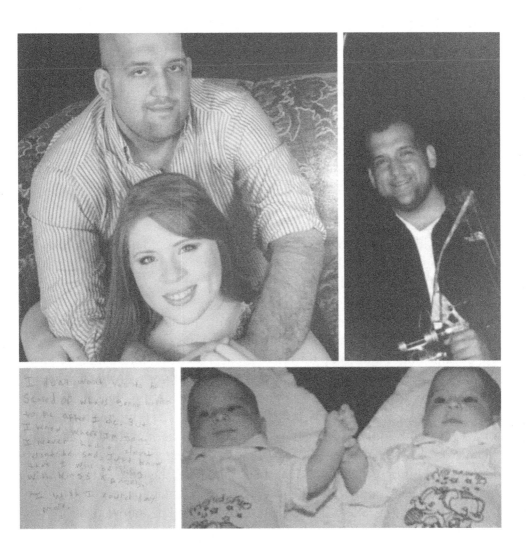

MARK EKLUND

David Gonzalez
New York State Corrections – Rikers Island Officer (Retired)

Writing this now as I sit in the Emergency Exit Isle - Seat 19C, five years later, on the same carrier, a JetBlue flight from JFK airport to LAS airport. On the way to the same show ISC- West, an International Security Show that I have attended for many years before and after this life changing event.

It was March 27th 2013. It seemed like just another trade show that I was traveling to like so many before. Unfortunately this would be one that stood out from the rest. I had taken several flight lessons into my pilot's license for small aircraft, which I will get to later.

Everything seemed normal until about an hour and a half into the early morning flight when a strange thing happened. The pilot's door opened and a pilot came out. I looked up towards the cockpit and an internal instinctual alarm went off. Where is the cart the flight attendant normally blocks the way to the front cabin bathroom as per protocol? Something inside made me sense that something was definitely wrong here. The Captain stood there for a few seconds looking down the isle towards the stern of the aircraft. He then made his way back to the rear bathroom. He entered and closed the door behind him. A flight attendant then came from the front of the cabin and went two isle seats behind me where another Captain, who was just off a Red Eye, was sitting. She said a few words to him and he followed her to the cockpit.

Meanwhile, only a few passengers who were awake, started to feel uneasy and watched for what may happen next.
The bathroom door flew open. The Captain stared towards the cockpit door and then started a brisk walk turning into a sprint at the same time yelling "Iraq, Iran… We have to get below 5,000 feet or it's going to explode". Most passengers were now aware but in disbelief that this was really happening.

The Co-Pilot called to the flight attendant to quickly go to the Red Eye pilot and have him get to the cockpit and change the code so the Captain couldn't get back in.

At this point, the Captain got to the door and stopped. He had a glazed look on his face like a deer in the headlights of an automobile. He then turns to the bathroom door and starts slamming on it "Let me in". The woman one row behind me had gone in the bathroom prior to all this starting and when he banged on the door, she screamed. She screamed so loud it startled the Captain that he stopped for a few seconds. He turned once again towards us down the isle then a few seconds later, turned to the cockpit door and slammed on it. Yes it was locked down but this Captain was about 6 foot 3 inches tall and 270 pounds. The top of the cockpit door flexed inward as each fist slammed on it. The lock held and he stopped for a few more seconds. Then over the PA system we heard "TAKE HIM DOWN!".

Now about ten guys got up simultaneously but David Gonzalez was the first to get to him as he was sitting in seat 1C. Being a former Corrections Officer, David had many years of experience and training on how to choke out a person to get them under control by making them pass out. Others were trying to grab him and keep him under restraint. The Captain was like a super human, adrenaline energized being that way, and he had to be taken out to ensure our safety. Once on the floor, the flight attendants grabbed the zip tie handcuffs stored on all aircraft, which they ended up using on his ankles.

When the Captain came back to consciousness, he began to wrestle with seven men trying to break free. They sat on him and pulled off their belts and hog tied him but remained on top of him as we emergency landed in Amarillo Texas at a small airport. Remember we are heading to an International Security Show so these folks onboard were from all walks of public safety and security and well trained to address an emergency. While all this was going on, we all watched the NEWS showing LIVE, our plane on the TV's headrests of the plane's seats. We also watched the military aircraft planes and helicopters following us until we landed.

After being taken off the plan in an orderly fashion, we were all interviewed by a seemingly large staff of investigators who took our statements.

Waiting as we are all briefed that the press will be seeking us out to get more information, I first got the chance to meet David and thanked him for saving all of us with the assistance of seven-plus other individuals.

When I asked him about the choke hold he put on the Captain, he said "As I was restricting his airflow, I could only think of my wife and kids and how I may get in big trouble for doing this as the Captain is a Federal employee and this could turn out bad and my life could be over"

But he instinctively did the right thing as we all know after the event. We all could have died that day.

David and I became close over the years. We get our families together from time to time and even work on security projects together.

The amazing thing about this life altering event is that there were people on this flight I had lost contact with for many years and we all bonded in a way you normally would not. It's still something we discuss when we bump into each other in the industry.

From a security standpoint, JetBlue followed the Emergency plan to the letter. They were very professional and open with us by keeping us informed.

I ended up stopping my flight lessons. I was encouraged to continue, but my passion to fly was gone. My life had changed a little that day.
Every time I board a flight I go on, I take time to observe all people's activities before and as we fly.

The appreciation I have sharpened from this event is like taking a bite from an apple whereas before the event, it was just an apple. Now every bite is delicious and important!

Mark Eklund

This HERO award is presented to David Gonzalez, who through physical training from his law enforcement career and heightened awareness training through ASIS International seminars, instinctually reacted during the crisis onboard JetBlue Flight 191 on March 27th, 2012 in which he selflessly aided in the saving of the lives of all on board.

MARSHALL MCCLAIN

The following oath from the film "Kingdom of Heaven" sums up
LAXPD Officer Tommy Edward Scott (EOW 4/29/2005) and the way he
walked this earth:

Be without fear in the face of your enemies.
Be brave and up right, that God may love thee.
Speak the truth always even if it leads to your death.
Safeguard the helpless and do no wrong.
That is your oath.
Arise a Knight.

The Kindest Officer on the Force
Tommy Scott, who was killed trying to stop a carjacker at LAX, was an
upbeat presence within the airport police department.
By Jennifer Oldham - Los AngelesTimes Staff Writer
May 7, 2005

I still remember the last time I saw him, after my tour of duty, graveyard
shift, as I walked to my car I saw him sitting alone in the field training
office. I said, "Tommy don't hurt him", he gave a loud laugh and said "Good
morning sir, you know I won't". You see if you knew Tommy you'd know that
was the biggest contradiction; Tommy was truly a kind soul with the rare
ability to make anyone instantly feel as though you've been lifelong friends.
The perfect combination of physical strength, passion for life and for people,
confident yet humble.

Tommy Scott, the first police officer to die in the line of duty in the 72-year
history of the Los Angeles Airport Police. Tommy embodied the essence
of a servant leader. He died at 35 years of age and more than half of his life
was in the service of others. For 15 years prior to joining the police force,
he worked for the Los Angeles Department of Recreation and Parks, part
of the time as a lifeguard, where he saved two children from drowning. In
under four years of graduating from the police academy, his work ethic and
leadership skills were noticeable, which lead him to being selected to several
assignments including being promoted to a Field Training Officer.

If you worked with Tommy, his personality didn't give much room for those who didn't consider themselves a morning person. Most mornings before the start of the 5:00 am morning watch roll-call, you would see some cops still wiping the sleep from their eyes or others clutching onto a cup of coffee to help pick them up before briefing started. Like clockwork, the door would be kicked in and Tommy would come bouncing in with a loud and boisterous "Good Morning Everyone!!!" Even those grumpy cops couldn't help but laugh every single time.

I cannot mention the man Tommy was without mentioning his father and best friend, Hubert Scott. Most of us met Mr. Scott after his son's untimely death and like his son, you quickly felt as though he was an old family friend or relative. Mr. Scott wanted to meet every person who knew and worked with his son. This amazing man spent more time consoling everyone and ensuring that every officer was ok, than focusing on his own loss. It was immediately made clear what we saw in Tommy was developed from simply following the model set by his father. Mr. Hubert Scott has since passed on but not without also leaving a lasting imprint on us all. His faith, his humor, his ethos matched that of ours, and his son Tommy embodied the primary LAXPD core value - Service before Self. We honor his memory and sacrifice with an annual charity run, which carries his name by way of a scholarship for all the children of airport employees.

Both Mr. Hubert and Tommy Scott had a profound impact on the airport police family. Everyone they encountered were left changed. Both are deeply missed and hold a place of honor.

How Heavy The Badge
How heavy the badge that hangs on my chest.
Sworn to protect and to serve, and to give all my best.

To find a lost child, or catch a bad guy.
So much responsibility, a brief pause and a sigh.

But the value of life, how much could it cost?
No one ponders that question, until a cop's life is lost.

And as for this poem, it now draws to an end.
Though LA's now safer, it cost me my friend.

- S. M. Smith (Los Angeles Airport Police Officer)

Marshall McClain

MATT PHILLIPS

A Family Tribute

My name is Matt Phillips and this is a brief recounting of some of my families participation in supporting this great nation in time of war.

My dad was born in 1915 and was the youngest of sixteen children, fourteen boys and two girls. I sometimes think that the two girls must have felt like indentured servants...

The family was a working family - my grandfather was the head gardener on J.P. Morgan's estate in Glen Cove, NY. All of the boys, at one time or another, worked on the estates that were along the North Shore of Long Island that was known as the, "Gold Coast".

When America went to war with the Kaiser of Germany in what was referred to as WW I, three of the boys enlisted in the service. One (Uncle Dink) went into the Navy, where he served on an old, "Four Stacker", Destroyer doing convoy escort duty in the Atlantic Ocean. The other two boys enlisted in the Army, and one (Uncle Perce) went overseas to fight in France with the 77th Infantry Division - known as the, "Statue of Liberty" Division. The 77th Infantry Division was organized with mostly of men from New York City and Long Island and trained at Camp Upton in the central part of Suffolk County, Long Island.

The 77th Infantry Division arrived in France in April 1918; overall it was the seventh of 42 divisions to reach the Western Front. The division fought in the Battle of Château-Thierry on 18 July 1918, and it was there that Uncle Perce was awarded a Silver Star for gallantry in action. He left that, and the original citation, with me and it has a place of honor in my study. Uncle Perce's service didn't stop there, he was a member of the Nassau County Police Dept. and rose to the rank of Commissioner, and also served as an Air Raid Warden during WW II.

When America entered WWII in 1941 after the 7 December bombing of Pearl Harbor by the Japanese, my dad was one of five that enlisted to serve - and my dad was the youngest at age twenty-six. And the oldest was my Uncle

Dink, who had also served in WW I with the Navy. He was an engineer for roads with the County of Nassau and re-enlisted in the Navy as a Seabee (construction Battalion) and served three years in the Pacific and participated in four campaigns. His last was on Okinawa where he ran into his son, Albert, who was also a Navy Seabee. He had another son, Bob, who was a torpedo man on a submarine, and a sister in law who was a US Army nurse stationed in Great Britain and then in the Pacific.

Two of the boys remained stateside with the USAAF. And the other, Art, was a communications specialist attached to the 101 Airborne in Europe. Meanwhile, my Grandmother sat home (granddad passed in 1942) and rolled bandages for the Red Cross with her flag with five stars on it hanging in the window.

My dad took a leave of absence from his job as a Policeman and enlisted in the Marine Corps in early 1942, and after boot camp in Paris Island, SC, he was sent to arial gunnery and radio school in Jacksonville, FL. He was then assigned to the 4th Marine Air Wing as a gunner/RTO (radio/telegraph operator) in an SBD Dauntless dive bomber. Dad was over twenty months in the Pacific, and participated in four campaigns (including landing as infantry in the battle of Peleliu) where his unit was awarded a Presidential Unit Citation (PUC). Dad always said that it was, "A million dollar experience that I wouldn't give you a nickel for today", and I had a small measure of understanding what he meant many years later in Iraq. And dad also continued serving after the war, returning to his job as a Police Officer on the Garden City Police where he retired as Chief of Police in 1976.

I, regretfully, could not serve in uniform as I had my right eye removed at age seven due to an injury. I ended up in the commodities trading industry - green coffee. The last fifteen years I was the President/CEO of the global headquarters of a Brasilian Agri Trading Company located on Long Island, which happened to be down the block from the Marine Corps First District Recruiting HQ. I befriended the Marines there and did all that I could to support them and their families.

When I retired in 2005, I wanted to do something more to directly support our military and so asked some of my friends that were senior officers if they could get me a deployment to Iraq in a logistical support position. In 2008, I deployed to Iraq as part of the OIF LOGCAP logistical support mission and worked out of Camp Liberty, outside of Baghdad for a few months. I then volunteered to forward deploy and was sent to Forward Operating Base Warrior in Kirkuk in the Kurdish region about 250 kilometers North of Baghdad, and worked with the Air Force personnel stationed there (they designated it KRAB - Kirkuk Regional Air Base) and the 10th Mountain division. Having the opportunity to see what great work our military personnel do, and in such miserable conditions, is what brought home dad's words to me - and I saw nothing that he and my Uncles saw or did. But I was pleased and proud to, at age 55, to have finally had the chance to make a minimal contribution in the legacy of our family's service.

And today I'm trying to support our wounded heroes from all branches of the service with my coffee company that is donating 50% of all profits to the non-for profit Semper Fi Fund. So the mission continues...

Social Media:
www.jarheadjava.com
www.facebook.com/jarheadjava

SOMETIMES PEOPLE DESERVE TO HAVE THEIR FAITH REWARDED...

Here at Jarhead Java, we donate 50% of all profits to the Semper Fi Fund and America's Fund - helping those from all branches of our military who have served and sacrificed.

HEAD OF NASSAU 100th WAR FAMILY LEAVES SON ON PACIFIC'S OKINAWA

Take a coffee break

MEAGHAN BREWINGTON

On February 21st, 2014, I, Meaghan, met my hero, Bernie Copeland who is a flight paramedic with the Air-Evac Lifeteam. Also, on that day, my life was completely turned around. The day started off as a normal day when I was a sophomore in high school. Once school let out, I decided to ride back home with my two friends. I sat behind Arriel, the driver. We decided to take some backroads. We turned onto a road called Rock House Hollow. As we turned onto the road, we started to speed up, went over the hill but ended up in the creek. We almost wrapped around a tree, due to another car coming in the opposite direction, and Arriel overcorrecting to the right. Going over that hill is when my whole life flashed before my eyes.

After the accident happened, both of my friends were mostly unharmed and were able to walk away from the scene safely. The car accident left me partially ejected out of the vehicle. I suffered critical injuries that left me fighting for me life. For example, I suffered from extreme fractures to my skull, facial bones on my left side being crushed, a fracture to my neck, bleeding on the brain in three spots, tearing a ligament in my knee, and several deep lacerations on my left hand and leg. Thus, I needed immediate help.

Fortunately, Bernie Copeland and his team came to my rescue, which altered my life forever. Due to a catastrophic injury to my jaw, the flight paramedics struggled to access an airway in my throat. However, Bernie was able to create an airway by inserting a tractotomy. In this moment of desperation, Bernie saved my life.

I arrived at Vanderbilt Hospital, a hospital located in Nashville, Tennessee, and needed to have several immediate surgeries to repair the damage done in the accident. I was immediately rushed to the trauma unit to have several surgeries done to reconstruct the damage to my face at the hospital. I then needed to stay in rehabilitation for two weeks to learn how to walk, talk, eat, and do anything a normal person would be able to do. The doctors predicted that it would take me about two years to fully recover from the injuries, especially the ones to the brain. They also said I likely would not graduate high school on time with my classmates. As I was told that news, I felt an overwhelming motivation to power through this horrific circumstance and prove the doctors wrong. Bernie also motivated me because he believed in me.

Bernie continued to get updates through my brother during my stay at Vanderbilt and has truly been an incredible support system for me since that day. Let me provide a few examples that stand out.

On May 23rd, 2014 I was invited to an EMS week cookout. This event is purely to honor first responders. This is where I finally got to meet the man who saved my life and start learning more about what it takes to become an inspiration. I also got to meet the rest of the team. Bernie showed me all the gear in the Air-Evac helicopter and he told me how special my story truly was. For example, he told me a lot about the accident and about how he wanted to ensure that I made it through okay.

I graduated high school on May 21st, 2016 right on time with my class and had scholarships to send me through college. Without Bernie's unmatched determination and passion for helping people, I would have never been able to make it as far as I have. Not only did Bernie help me during the accident, but he also came to see me walk across the stage at my graduation ceremony. It meant so much to me that he used his limited free time to come witness that day. I am not one to have a big group of friends, but to have him there said more than anything. He has always believed in me and has always supported me.

 He will still ask how I am doing and, in my opinion, that is what truly defines him as an inspiration. He not only reached out during my time at the hospital, but he also wants to see me succeed in life. When I think of the word hero, without hesitation, the first person I think of is Bernie Copeland. He truly has a passion for what he does and has motivated me to work towards a career in the medical profession. There are not enough words I can say to be able to thank him for what and all he has done for me. He is the most selfless life coach someone could be blessed with. I can only hope to make half the impact on someone as he did on me in my future career, and to be able to change lives the way he has changed mine.

In closing, Bernie is a person that deserves such honor. Without him, I would not be here along with the other patients that he has helped impact. This man has changed the way I see the world. I now see a world where dreams can happen and where differences can be made in people's lives. Someone who was originally a stranger has now become one of my greatest inspirations. Thank you Bernie, for all the differences you have made and will make in my life and in others.

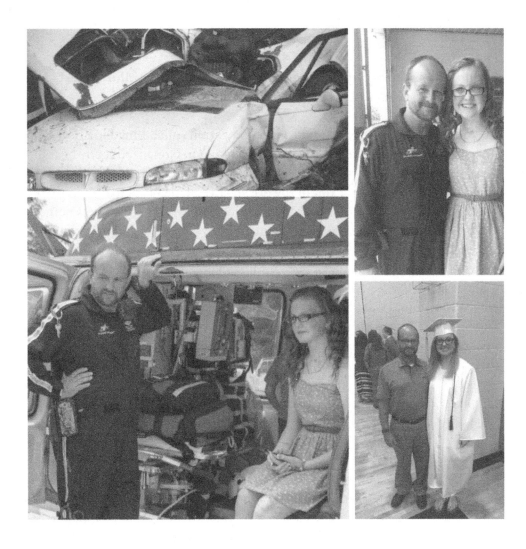

MEGAN O'GRADY

Steven McDonald
New York City Police Department
1986-2017
Detective
I honored his service by making teddy bears out of his uniform shirts for his wife, Patti Ann and his son, Conor.

In January 2017 I created a nonprofit organization called Blue Line Bears to honor fallen law enforcement officers by making personalized teddy bears out of their uniform shirts to give to their children and families. Although it is hard to choose only one out of the dozens I've made bears to honor, there is one special officer whose story left a lasting impression on me. His name is Steven McDonald. He passed away just 10 days after I began my nonprofit, and little did I know at the time how he would change my life. My dad, a police officer himself, knew of Steven McDonald and his story which began many years before I was even born. In his first months as an officer, Detective Steven McDonald was shot while working in Central Park. He almost died from his injuries and ended up paralyzed from the neck down and he relied on a respirator for 31 years. Most people would have harbored hatred toward the man who shot them and want to get revenge. However, this wasn't how Detective McDonald lived. Instead, he forgave the young man who shot him and even became friends with him. He then spent the rest of his life spreading his message of forgiveness to others around the world.

Steven McDonald's life is nothing short of a miracle. When I was asked to make bears in his memory, my life changed. I didn't know his story until I had the honor of meeting his family. His wife and son welcomed me into their home and showed me every part that was special to Detective McDonald. His room was full of rosaries, crosses, and items people all over the world had given him. Patti Ann even gave me a teddy bear that was very special to him. The purpose of this, however, isn't to talk about what was given to me physically; but rather to talk about what Steven spiritually gave me. He showed me the importance of faith. He showed me you never know when your life will change, good or bad so you just have to thank God for the life he has given you, the breaths he gives you, the love he has for you. He showed me how God has so much love for you that he will challenge you to be the best you can be, but you have to weather the storms of darkness in order to fully understand that love. He taught me forgiveness is a simple action that is perceived as difficult, but can change your life and the lives of others including those who have hurt you. He showed me family is more important than anything else this life can physically give you. Family is where the love is and family is important for the heart. Lastly, from a poem he wrote titled "You Are Very Special" he reminded me we are all different in this world. This is important because it makes us who we are. We are all given the choice to choose good or evil and it is up to us to choose the good. We must all choose to be the force the devil cannot control. It is up to us to be the good in the world and make it the best place we can possibly make it. I know Steven McDonald is watching me every day, and I know he will live forever in the hearts of those who are good people. Thank you, Detective McDonald, for changing my life for the better.

Megan O'Grady

http://www.bluelinebears.org
Facebook Blue Line Bears
Twitter@bluelinebears

Michael & Roxann Cotugno

In July 2013, I met one of the strongest, inspiring young man that I have
ever met in my life. Ret. Spec Justin P Lane aka "JP." JP joined the military
in 2008 and in 2010 he was deployed to Afghanistan. His job was one of the
most dangerous ones of all. He was to go and search for IED's. (Improvised
explosive devices) On July 2, 2011, JP was blown up 3 times, the last one
almost ended his life. JP was in a coma for 6 weeks and when he woke up,
he was missing both his legs, a few fingers, had a tracheotomy, his pelvis
was dislocated, and most of his torso was destroyed by shrapnel. His life was
completely changed. The doctors said he would have speech problems and he
would never be able to sing.

JP told me he knew why he didn't die out there that day. God had a mission
for him. JP continued to prove the doctors wrong and he started walking
with prosthetics. He became the only double amputee recording artist in the
world. He has traveled all over the US, has preformed at two Presidential
Inaugurations, and has traveled all over Mexico & Brazil performing and
inspiring thousands of people.

JP's attitude is never give up, never surrender. He might have retired from
the military but he has never stop serving. He performs for non-profit
Veteran Service Organizations, he is a Veteran Celebrity Ambassador for
Adapt A Vet, he serves meals to the homeless under the bridge, and he goes
to different schools and talks with young adults. Every time I listen to him
give a motivational speech, I watch the crowds react when he finishes his
story. You can hear the crowd talking about how their life really isn't that
bad after all, and that their own problems are not bad after hearing JP's story.
You could be having the worst day of your life, listen to JP speak and your
dreadful day wouldn't be that bad any more. He has away of inspiring people
by just being around them.

Two years ago, JP had to have another surgery on one of his thighs, while he
was in surgery I wanted to do something special for him. My husband and I
went and met with a legend, Country music artist, Merle Haggard, and had
him autograph a guitar for JP. That evening when we arrived at the hospital,
several of the doctors and nurses asked me if JP was going to sing. I said he
just had surgery but if he feels up to it I would let them all know. After JP saw

his guitar, he forgave me for not being at the hospital when he woke up. He asked me to invite all the doctors and nurses into his room, so he could give them a mini concert. No matter what JP has going on in his own life, he is always wanting to serve others and make a difference in their life.

JP met the perfect woman for him in February 2017. In a short amount of time, we all knew she was the one for him. They have so much in common, have the same beliefs, and they completed each other. March of 2018 JP and Crystal were married. We have an incredible daughter in-law, they just got their first fur baby and we can't wait for them to make us grandparents. Now JP & Crystal work together inspiring couples around them, telling the amazing story of what brought them together. Together they feed the homeless, volunteer to help Veterans, and speak to youth all over the US.

JP could have chosen to accept what the doctors said and not follow his dreams and just sit around feeling sorry for himself but instead he reached for the stars.

There is no way I could say thank you enough to JP for signing on the dotted line, for fighting for our freedom, for fighting to stay alive, for becoming apart of our lives, for completing us, for sharing his dreams, his success, his love and his new family.

Thank you, JP, for all you are and all you do for everyone. You are an amazing man and we are honored that you chose us to be your Texas parents. We love you.

Michael and Roxann Cotugno
Adapt a Vet
www.adaptavet.org
Facebook Adapt A Vet
Twitter @adaptavet

MICHAEL POTORTI

Support Your First Responders

September 10, 2001. I just got off the 4 Train at Fulton St. to head over to my Manhattan office at Two World Financial Center (next to World Trade Center). It was a beautiful crisp fall day and I remember looking up at the towers before I entered the bridge that took me to my office. "Wow" I said.

Next day the world changed. I decided not to go into the office that day and prepare for a training I had to teach in Atlanta the following week. I went into the gym in the morning and heard the radio announcer say that a plane flew into one of the Twin Towers. "Maybe a small plane went off course "I thought. I went home and turned on the TV, only to see one of the towers collapsing. It was surreal. What was happening?
Then I saw video of people running out of the towers while Firefighters and Police were running in.

This is a testament to the stuff that First Responders are made of. More video came out in the weeks and months ahead that showed First Responders carrying people around, comforting others who were hysterical, hosing down the fire and smoke which billowed out of the debris that was once Two Glorious Towers.

I will never forget that day and those Super Human First Responders. When I see and hear news clips of people protesting entire police departments because of a few "bad apples" I really get incensed. These men and women enter into the life of protector knowing there is a risk that they won't return home to their families in the evening. I have two cousins who are Sergeants in the NYC Police Department – one is stationed in the South Bronx and the other in Manhattan. When I heard on the radio that a Police Sergeant was shot and killed in the Bronx a few years ago, I had a lump in my throat. I immediately texted my Aunt and she said everyone was OK. Imagine what she felt when she heard the news…

Fast Forward to April, 12, 2012. I was with my daughter in the car heading off to Canada for a wedding when we stopped for the night in NY halfway. We were having dinner and I noticed on TV that there was a big Police scene in Greenland, NH – we lived next door in Stratham. I called home to see what was going on and the police had closed down Route 33 and told everyone to stay indoors. "What is going on?" I thought. Further news revealed that Chief Michael Maloney of the Greenland Police Department was killed trying to protect his fellow officer brothers from a deranged shooter related to a drug bust. Chief Maloney was a 26 year veteran and was only a few days from retirement. He could have let others handle the situation but went into the situation and made the ultimate sacrifice.

This is another testament to the fabric of these First Responders. A few years later we opened the Beara Brewing Co. in Portsmouth NH. We collected Police and Firemen sleeve patches and put them up on the wall. Since then we have received a load of patches from customers who noticed them. Chief Maloney's sister came in and asked that we put a picture of him up on the wall as well. "He would have loved your beer" she said. I also ran a couple of the Chief Maloney 10K's which raises money for the Chief Michael Maloney Memorial Fund that provides charitable services to the Seacoast of New Hampshire's First Responders.

"What else can I do for them?" I thought. An idea popped into my head to make a special batch of brew in his honor, sell it, and give the proceeds to the Fund. We had loads of local media attention and launched it in a special event on a Friday eve. We ended up donating over $1,000 to the Fund.

That's what community is all about. Honoring your First Responders and what they do to keep you and your family safe. So the next time you see a First Responder, shake his or her hand and say "Thank you for what you do." They will appreciate it.

Michael Potorti, Founder/Brewer – Beara Brewing Co.
www.bearairishbrew.com
www.facebook.com/BearaIrishBrewingCo
www.instagram.com/bearairishbrew/?hl=en
twitter.com/BearaIrishBrew

Minitwabe Ademe

LA county Lennox sheriff department
7/11/2018

Sheriff,

He was an utter stranger who was being a good Samaritan but to me and my sister, he was like a guardian angel.

This deputy Sheriff showed me that acts of kindness that can seem minor, can have a significant impact on a person's life, this was true in my case.

It was the summer of 1988, I was 13 and my sister was 15 years old. Around 9pm that evening, we decided to run away from home due to the strict home environment that my parents readily reinforced. Not realizing the danger, we had an encounter with two suspicious men following us in old car with dark tinted windows. Sensing danger, we tried to avoid them and quickly tried to walk to the nearest shopping center hoping that a crowd would deter them to leave us alone. As we neared the shopping center, we saw this deputy Sheriff and approached him to let him know about these potential child predators. But when we surveyed the area, we noticed that the vehicle was gone. As we explained the entire situation (including why we were walking out on the streets), the officer identified the severity of the situation and demanded our address and parent's information. With our family's military background, we were always taught to trust and respect our elders and people in uniform. This served us well as this deputy Sheriff was kind, protective, and empathic to our plight. Even though he was technically off duty, he escorted us home and stayed to speak with our parents as he understood the fear we had by returning home.

When we returned home, our parents and oldest sister were waiting in front as our brothers had been sent to comb the neighborhood to find us. To my surprise, my father was not angry. He only wanted to thank the officer for returning us home. I am certain that the officer and my parents exchanged information but that was never passed along to us. Now that my parents are gone, I have regret that I never got an opportunity to let him see how his action affected my life. Knowing that I have life today and that I now have children of my own is just a testimony to his action that day. That day could have ended up tragically for two young girls if he chose not to get "involved". This is a wonderful example of how lives can be impacted by one single person's decision to care about a stranger and to take time to get involved and make a difference. I feel like I owe my and my sister's life to this individual. I hope one day he understands the impact of his actions that day.

This officer was a true man, a man who did more than he could have imagined, a man who protected two girls at their lowest point, a guardian in my eyes and a true hero. I would extend my gratitude to all the sheriffs in LA County and every first responder who are out there protecting our communities everywhere.

Sincerely yours,
Minitwabe Ademe

PAULA SCHLEPPI

Calling Car 51, Calling Car 51

His journey you see
All started pre-me
USMC Military
There it was born
His desire to be sworn
As an officer of the law

His 1st dream came true
A member of the blue
A Columbus Police Auxillary
He was not tall enough unfortunately
To be all he really wanted be

A blackbird waiting for his moment to arise
And then he found
Much too his surprise
His home nest
Where he could be like the rest

He became all he wanted to be
A full time officer of the law
With the Bexley City PD

Through the years
It was not all
Peaches n' cream
Just his dream
There were cheers
There were jeers
There were tears
But, he took it all in stride
He stood his post with much pride

As a little girl

I often wondered
Would my daddy
Be there in the morning
To sing to me
You are my sunshine, my only sunshine
Will he be here tonight
To hold me tight
& recite
I love you
& then tuck me in tight
& yell back "don't let the bed bugs bite"
As he exited the bedroom door for the night

Then there was the CB
Ringing out morning, noon & night
I remember many plights
But the one so chilling
always would be
The one we hated hearing

"Calling car 51"
"Calling car 51"
It was his calling
He was a man of valor
He did his duty
1st shift, 2nd shift, 3rd shift
He was on call hour by hour
Because you see
A Policeman is always a Policeman & will always be

He was a son, a brother, a friend, an uncle, a husband, a father, a grandfather.
But most of all he was a mentor. He gave a gift, the gift of light & life to
many. His utmost goal for you & me alike was to keep you safe from harm &
teach those in need, right from wrong.

To this day, I love, honor and respect each and every one of you…the
brothers, the sisters and the families in blue.

USMC 1955 – 1961

Bexley Ohio City Police 1969 – 1995
Badge #S1
Car 51
Sergeant Roger L. Sluder Sr.

ROBERT DILLON

A TRIBUTE TO MY SON, SCOTT LOUIS DILLON

As a little boy around three years old, my son, Scotty, was fascinated with fire trucks. He joined the local volunteer fire dept. in Uniontown, Ohio where we lived when he was still in high school.

He moved on after graduation from Lake High School, and after he was married, he worked various jobs in Canton, Ohio. He joined Plain Twp. Fire Dept. as a volunteer. After he was with them for a while, he became an EMT (emergency medical technician) He loved his job of helping people, along with putting out fires.

A few years later, he and his wife had two boys (Joshua and Nicholas) whom he loved even more than the fire dept. Scott never turned down the opportunity to be in a parade. His two boys would be right there on the fire truck with him when they were permitted.

One day he heard about a full time firefighter's job in the Brecksville, Ohio VA Fire Dept. He got the job and had to drive some distance to work. He worked 24 hours on duty and 48 hours off. This was hard on his family because every fourth day Scott had to pull duty at the fire station. He was finally making a decent wage but it was tough being away from his family that he loved so much.

He was in a situation at work where there was a chemical spill in the garage area. Scott was first in the building to check it out. As soon as he entered the area he blacked out and was taken to the hospital. Doctors indicated he had damage to his lungs from the chemical. This ended his dream and career as a firefighter.

To serve others, he chose to apply for training at the University of Akron's Police Academy. He joined the force at the Cleveland Metro Health Hospital. He really enjoyed helping people. He was dedicated to his job for a year.

The VA Hospital chemical spill resulted in a lymphoma diagnosis at age 40. He fought cancer until he was 54 years old and lost the battle. All four of his children will carry on his legacy.

I enjoyed all the years of hunting, fishing, building a dune buggy together and many more things we shared together. He truly was my best buddy through all the years I had him. Jesus has him now, and I will be with him when I meet my Savior Jesus.

I love you son,
Your dad.
(Robert Dillon)

Ron Darling

Rudy

An 18 year old boy from Thomas Idaho, drafted in 1944 leaves basic training and steps off the bus in New York City. Rulon Grant Van Orden, known as Rudy, had never seen anything like this. Two days later after buying souvenirs for his family, that the stores never shipped as promised, he boards the Queen Elizabeth with something like 7,000 other G.I.'s headed for England. The trip over was one that consisted of using his Idaho farm boy smarts. Sequestered to a lower deck, where everyone was sea sick and throwing up all over, he quickly realized the only way he could survive this trek without getting sick himself was to sneak up on the deck. Punishment for going to the deck before his groups turn would have been severe had he been caught, but he was never caught. He spent the majority of his time on deck dodging officers and men in charge. Arriving in London, they prepared for the channel crossing. D-Day had been just weeks before and his platoon was to be inserted as replacements in the Battle of the Bulge. After watching the moving saving Private Ryan with him, and seeing how somber he was as we left the theater, I asked him how many days had been like those last three of Private Ryan's, he paused, thought for a few seconds and responded… "well, I was there for 194 days, so probably 192 days like that." He went on to tell that they were shelled by German artillery every day and every night non-stop. One time as we were watching the mini-series Band of Brothers, he commented how lucky those first line guys were. He said…yeah, they had it rough, but they got days off. As replacements, we got there when things were not going so well, and we never got one single day off.

He told of the bitter cold fighting in Belgium and Germany, how his platoon lost more men to injury from foot rot and frost bite than to German bullets. He learned early on to always carry an extra two pair of socks, one tucked under each arm pit. The cold was almost unbearable for many of the men. Lots of them grew up in Texas and Southern states and they were not used to the bitter cold. Growing up in Eastern Idaho, Rudy was built for the cold.

He told the story of being pinned down by a group of German snipers, and hiding behind the trees which, even though they were in a wood forest, were all planted in straight lines. Something very odd for a kid from the mountains of Idaho where everything was still, natural and wild. They were hiding behind trees to keep from getting shot, standing, using the trees to block the German's view of them. One private kept peeking out, looking to see where the Germans were hiding, hoping to get a shot off. Rudy told him to quit peeking out, and sure enough a few minutes later the soldier peeked out again and a round hit his helmet and took a chunk of the guy's head off. He was alive, and they were able to pack the wound with snow and somehow got him out and headed to the medical station a few miles back. Rudy did not know what happened to that guy for many years. One day his phone rang in about 1990 and it was that guy. He said he had been trying to find him all that time to thank him. He said after Rudy warned him, he didn't lean out as far. Had he leaned out as far as he had been, he would have been killed. He credited Rudy for saving his life.

After just a few short weeks, they had lost so many men in his platoon that he ended up being the most senior and received a field promotion to Sergeant. He was not happy about that because that meant he would be carrying a machine gun and the Germans targeted the guys with machine guns first. He also had a tough time shooting directly at any German…even though he knew they were trying to kill him. He grew up L.D.S. (Mormon) and he valued life highly, plus his Mother had escaped Germany shortly after WWI, and he knew that some of the soldiers he was shooting at could be his cousins, or family of some sort. He said he never did take direct aim, rather he would just spray an area and not focus on any one enemy soldier.

He told of being shelled one particular time when the shelling had been going for several days non-stop. Usually there would be a few hours when there was no incoming…not these last few days he would say. He told that you could tell when the shells were getting close. There was a whistle as they would come in, then if they were not real close, whistle boom. If they were close whistle, then a couple seconds of silence followed by whoosh of air. When they went silent you knew it could be your time. One shell was coming in, went silent, and he and his buddy dove into a fox hole. After the shell went off only a few feet away Rudy ask his friend why he had kicked him. They guy started laughing and said, I didn't kick you…look at your helmet. He had taken shrapnel from the blast and it had hit his helmet and peeled the top back like a sardine can. He said he wanted to save it as a souvenir, but they were too heavy to carry an extra one.

Once they reach Germany, they fought only a couple more weeks and the war ended. He was stationed in Munich and was assigned an old German man to care for. The man had been the mayor of Munich before the war. He had been anti Hitler and had been imprisoned. He was old and died while Rudy was caring for him. The man wrote a will before he died and left all his worldly belongings to Rudy because his family was all dead and Rudy had treated him so kind. The only stipulation was that Rudy had to remain in Germany to take ownership. He found out later, after he declined…he just wanted to go home, that the man owned one square block of downtown Munich.

While in Germany, he looked up his Mother's sister and his cousins. They lived in Klon. He finally found them and took them a box of rations. He knew the German people were starving. He spoke no German and they spoke no English but he eventually got them to understand that he was their nephew/cousin, that Wilhelmina Stubelson was his mother. They had a great time and spent several days together.
He was given the option to go to the Pacific theater, or to go home. If he chose home, he would lose his field commission and be returned to being a corporal. He chose to go home.

Rulon Grant Van Orden was my best friend, my Father in Law for over 42 years and the man more responsible for the man I became than any other on this planet. He was the best of the best, a man I owe everything to. He passed from this world at age 92 in December of 2016. I look forward to being re-united with him in the next life to take up where we left off.

He lived with my wife and I and his wonderful bride, the girl one year ahead of him in High School that he had a crush on, the one who married and had two children, then divorced, and he found her and made her his own. They had four children together and my wife was one of those. They lived with us the last five years of their lives, they passed 47 days apart, she went first. It broke his heart and he could not go on without her. The last few days, he lost his ability to communicate with words. He refused to have a bowel movement in his adult diaper and so sometimes in the middle of the night he would make enough noise he would wake me, and I would have to get him out of bed, and into his wheel chair…the last few weeks he had lost his ability to stand and walk. Two nights before he passed this happened. He had not been able to talk for almost a week. I lifted him into the wheel chair, took him to the bathroom and lifted him onto the toilet where he fell asleep. I woke him and ask if he was finished three times, each time a grunt and shaking of the head saying no. The last time, he looked me in the eye and said…why? Are you in a hurry? His last words to me, after not speaking for almost a week. He was able to tell my wife he loved her the next day and the day after that, he was gone when we woke up.

I told that last part, to show you the love I had for that man…I would have done anything for him. Having him and Nancy's (my wife) Mom with us that last five years was a privilege and joy I will never forget.

He was the greatest man I ever met.

Ron Darling

ROSE LEES

This passage is dedicated to a man that has had a tremendous impact on my life. My brother-in-law Matthew Fayette.

Matthew Fayette is a man that is filled to the brim with courage, leadership, and loyalty. I am so very thankful that he has become a leading influence in my life. His kind, protecting, patriotic, and tenacious personality has carried him far through life. When he was younger, after he graduated from his pilot training introductory class, at the age of only 16, Fayette received a pair of silver pilot wings. To him this signified what he dreamed to be in the future, a pilot.

His journey with the Military began in 2006, when he joined the United States Air Force. In 2007, Fayette became a TACP. The Tactical Air Control Party, commonly abbreviated TACP, is a small team of Air Force, or Marine personnel who provide airspace deconfliction and terminal control of close air support at battlegroup level or below.
"We arrived at our little outpost in mid December 2007. It was in the middle of nowhere, surrounded by mountains, just a stone throw away from Pakistan. We got settled in and it was pretty calm for a while. I was part of a two man team from the Air Force. Our job was to go on patrols and missions with soldiers from the 173rd Airborne Brigade on the ground, and coordinate air strikes with Air Force fighter jets, when we started getting shot at. The mountains were covered in snow, so the insurgents didn't launch many attacks in the winter. The snow was hard to walk through, and they would leave tracks, letting us know where they went once they retreated", Matt remarked.

"Spring, commonly known in Afghanistan as 'fighting season', finally rolled around. Through the different missions and ambushes on our outposts, I had bullets pass within inches of my body; RPG's impact so close that the noise of the explosion was muffled by the sound of shrapnel buzzing by my head like giant bumble bees. Before too long, we got used to getting shot at, and functioning very well in the middle of it all. A large number of the attacks were pretty ineffective, we heard machine guns going off, but couldn't see or hear any rounds coming near us. Those ineffective attacks were annoying and lead to complacency on our part. Faced with months of fighting, in the most violent corner of Afghanistan, we all had to accept that there is a real possibility of not coming home. Once you accept death, you can push the fear side, and focus on doing your job as well as you can, doing your best to keep everyone else alive", he said.

He spent the remainder of 2007 and the majority of 2008 in Afghanistan. The rest of his deployment was spent in Europe executing various exercises with NATO partners. NATO, the North Atlantic Treaty Organization, is a military alliance of European and North American democracies founded after World War II to strengthen international ties between member states—especially the United States and Europe—and to serve as a counter-balance to the Soviet Union and the Warsaw Pact.

His time spent in the Air Force was not only full of rigorous training but was also laced with new "fun" activities. Before his deployment ended, he had the opportunity to fly in an F-16. Not only did he have the opportunity to fly over Venice, but also flew just a couple hundred feet about the rolling vineyards south of Venice. "That kept me motivated to continue to pursue a career in piloting", he mentioned.

My decision to attend the University of Eastern Michigan for academics and to attend the University of Michigan for AFROTC training was highly influenced by Matt. He sat down with me at the recruiting station, spoke with me about different positions, and helped me choose a position that would help me obtain the skills needed for my future with a medical outreach program called Doctors Without Borders. Several members of my family were able to attend his graduation from Officer Training School in Montgomery, Alabama, in the month of November, 2017. When my quadruplet brother Nevin walked with me onto the grass to congratulate Matt, we couldn't have been more proud. We both had the honor of pinning on his 2nd Lieutenant bars on his uniform lapels.

He met with the two of us later, individually, to tell us about how he was inspired when he was younger. Those silver pilot wings he received when he was 16, were his greatest inspiration and he would turn to them for encouragement whenever he doubted his future as a pilot for the Air Force. He then presented both Nevin and I with a 2nd Lieutenant pin for us each to have as inspiration for our futures in the Marines and Air Force respectively. I put that pin on the strap of my college backpack and I look at it every day as inspiration to complete my AFROTC and medical courses. I look forward to serving this great country in the very near future.

Rose Lees

SHEILA BROWN

Hat's off to Long Beach California
* Special Engine 17 *

On the 3rd of February this year, 2018, me and my son Robert (36) moved out of our apartment we shared for the past 17 years and were set to move in at his father's home and would be occupying it for the next year. As a special treat for my son Robert, I rented a room at The Hotel Current in Long Beach, California and planned on pampering him with room service, pedicure, manicure and most of all, he could actually sit down in a shower for as long as he would like to.

My son Robert is one of the kindest and most enjoyable and just a super duper son, grandson, brother, nephew, uncle anyone could ever ask for. He's just seemed to have lost his way since he took a fall at work four years ago and has been out on disability which ran out two years ago and has put on more than 200 pounds. His weight is approximately 650 pounds and has taken a toll on him as to why I wanted this pampering to be given to him on February 3rd, 2018.

Unfortunately when we arrived at the Hotel Current, I took some things into the room from his truck and came right back out to assist with him. He was on the other side of his truck one second and in a blink of an eye, he was gone. I no longer saw him standing there. I yelled out to him and I heard nothing, so I ran around the truck and there he was on the ground!!! It literally broke my heart to see him sitting there with tears in his eyes because he was too heavy to get himself up.

I tried to help him up but all it did was hurt his arm. I was so worried someone was going to pull into the spot where he landed which was a vacant parking spot in-between two cars…I instantly called his father to come help. He arrived but neither one of us could get him up. I ran to the office to have the manager call for fire department for help.

Engine 14 arrived and after several minutes went by, no one was able to get him up due to his weight. I'm in heartbreak and in tears besides angry at the very busy hotel occupants wanting to look and whisper but I kept my composer to only my son….no one else mattered.

It took one of the best firemen (in my book), I only wish I could have remembered his name, to think of calling out "Special Engine 17" who has equipment to take up to 5000 pounds of whatever it may be, a car, bricks, or metal off of people in accidents. After it arrived, it was something so amazing as a flat round rubber piece approximately 5 feet in diameter (round) blue in color and they got it under my son and little by little it inflated with air and rose him off the round, and he grabbed on to the side of his truck and, walla, he was up and standing….in my book…Special Engine 17 Rocks!!!

They saved my son from being on the ground for over two hours and my broken heart.

Hat's off to Long Beach California Special Engine 17 *

Sheila Brown

STEPHANIE CROSS

Tribute to: RONALD JAMES HUGHES

Memorializing your Dad is something no little girl is ever prepared to do, but like others who serve selflessly, my Dad deserves it. I hope this lump in my throat does not obstruct his story or my words.

My Father, Ronald James Hughes was born on December 28th, 1937 in W. Stewartstown, New Hampshire. He left me so many things when he passed on February 25th, 2016 of congestive heart failure. By things, I mean, traits, characteristics, stories, and memories. He was, and shall remain, my hero.

Dad took interest in being on the local Colebrook, New Hampshire Fire Department at 18 years old, but patiently wailed uphill at age 23 in 1960 to be given a spot in the department. He served Colebrook Fire Department and held about every position and then retired as Chief in 1998.

Thirty eight selfless years of giving back to our small North Country town of under 3000 residents. A retirement gathering in January of 1998 revealed to me that my Dad had impacted the entire North Country and all of New England. Firefighters and EMS from all over the area attended, and we learned of his many contributions to not only to our immediate community, but the entire State of New Hampshire where he was given many accolades for being a member of the New Hampshire Fire Chiefs' Association and doctrine contributor to the New Hampshire State Fire Academy where he is still revered today.

Dad was drafted into the Army serving from 1961 – 1963 and service was something he never shirked. He was born a teacher, leader, and served with pride. My brothers and I can recall countless important lessons he has instilled. These life lessons shape every facet of our lives, and he left us the ability and willingness to serve in many capacities and care about our communities. We are always grateful to his loving example. I recall asking him upon retirement in 1998 if he thought it would be hard not answering the call when the scanner toned out a call. His reply still is a point of reference for life I cannot forget. He said, "Steph, if I did my best in this position, there will be many following behind that will be ready to step into this role".

Dad didn't even retain a scanner in the house to hear where and when the fires were. I remember watching intently though. On occasion when our town's "noon whistle" signaled a fire with repeated blows, and he would sit forward in his chair, heart racing, imaging and knowing all well the sirens meaning.

When my Dad passed away and throughout his wake and burial service, so many people paid their respects, showing stories of the man I knew as Dad, and we learned he had impacted, served, and touched so many. The funeral home was a tribute and memorial in itself as Engine 2 was parked out front proudly with his turn-out gear and with his Fire Chief's hat sitting on the bumper. I am a lucky daughter and the lessons and years my father gave of himself to our community taught me the importance of serving a cause greater than oneself. At the close of his wake, the tones went off and a fire was called out breaking into our sadness at his casket. In my heart, I knew it was Dad's way of saying, remember me but let life go on and make it count! So my commitment to his memory and lifelong take away is to love life, give back, and serve others because it truly matters.

RIP Dad – you are missed every second of every hour of every day.

STEPHANIE CROSS

In Loving Memory

Ronald J. Hughes

Dec. 28, 1937 – Feb. 25, 2016
78 Years of Age

When I must leave you for a little while,
please do not grieve and shed wild tears
and hug your sorrow to you
through the years.
But start out bravely with a gallant smile,
and for my sake and in my name live on
and do all things the same.
Feed not your loneliness on empty days
but fill each waking hour in useful ways.
Reach out your hand in comfort and in
cheer and I in turn will comfort you
and hold you near.
And never, never be afraid to die,
for I am waiting for you in the sky.

STEPHANIE SALB

Sergeant David Alexander McLean, Jr.
United States Marine Corps—1965-1970
Stationed in Vietnam, Cuba and stateside
Currently residing in Holly Springs, NC/Senior Pastor at Fellowship of
Christ Church, Cary, NC
Submitted by: Stephanie Salb/sister-in-law

It was 1965. The counter-culture was underway, the Vietnam conflict was worsening and the Civil Rights movement exploding. As if sync with the upheaval around him, David McLean, Jr. was 17 and restless. Born in 1947 in the Belgian Congo to American missionary parents who served there at the time, following in his father's ministry footsteps was something David had no desire to do. College was not for him either; staying at home was not an option. David decided to volunteer for the military and as he was still a minor, with his parents' written permission, the US Marine Corp welcomed him. He married his girlfriend just before leaving for boot camp and soon he learned that he had a child on the way.

After boot camp, his first assignment was Vietnam, where he would be assigned for nineteen months. As intense as Vietnam was, David says his actual worst day in the military was his first day of boot camp. Once he survived that, he knew what he was made of, and it would enable him to meet the challenges of the conflicts that lay ahead. David would be stationed in Dong Ha, the mountainous region south of the demilitarized zone.

While his boot camp training had prepared him well for the conflict in Southeast Asia, David was not particularly close to God at the time. It may be surprising (or not) that the son of missionary parents found himself disengaged from the church and its teachings, particularly when he had had a good relationship with his mother and father. The spiritual path is an individual one, though, and David just wasn't feeling it. Even with the chaos and terror of the war raging around him, he did not call out to the Lord for help or to pray with the exception of the times he was in foxholes. The saying is that every soldier is a Christian in a foxhole but on one occasion, David found himself next to an atheist who was screaming out that there was no God and if there were one, He wouldn't rescue them. David and his soldier buddy Rich Nyce (who would become a lifelong friend) told the guy to shut up or they would toss him out into the crossfire. The man shut up.

Instead of turning his eyes upward for strength, David found himself turning to recreational drugs for relief from the intensity of war, as did many of his fellow soldiers. It was the beginning of a decision he would come to regret.

He shared many of the frustrations of the other men serving in the conflict that the U.S. government refused to call a war. The soldiers were constantly being restrained from taking any kind of aggressive action that would violate the rules of war, since they technically were not engaged in a war. When fighting would break out, the men often found that the South Vietnamese soldiers, whom they were protecting and assisting, would quickly abandon them, leaving the Americans to fight alone. Back in the States, of course, the U.S. government's leadership of the Vietnam conflict was collapsing due to political infighting and its refusal to let the military commanders have the decision making authority they needed to win the conflict on the ground. The government attempted to conceal the divisiveness from the troops, but the soldiers were well aware of what was going on back home, both in the government that was failing them and the growing anti-war movement among the youth, says David.

After his tour in Vietnam ended, he was stationed in Guantanamo Bay, Cuba for three months and then back home stateside. By the time he left the Marines in 1970, he had been promoted to the rank of sergeant.

As a former Marine in an unpopular war, David quickly learned that he and his "brothers" were unfairly scape-goated by a large segment of the American population that did not appreciate the efforts of the men and women of the U.S. military. They were warned to not publicly wear their uniforms, particularly in California, where servicemen had even been shot at. It was a bitter disappointment to be betrayed by the country he had put his life on the line for. The sacrifices that David and his fellow soldiers made, many of them resulting in the ultimate sacrifices of their lives, seemed in vain. Many years later, an acquaintance who had formerly worked in intelligence revealed to David that the American efforts in Vietnam had actually paid off invaluably because many other countries who had been on the brink of Communism had been deterred because of the United States presence in Southeast Asia. In the early 70's, though, that truth was not yet known and the rejection by

David's fellow countrymen, many of whom had refused to serve, stung hard.

David found himself turning more and more to illegal drugs not just to numb the pain but in his quest to find greater meaning for his life. By now, he and his wife had divorced, adding another layer of sadness to his world.

During the tumultuous early 1970's, he found a positive outlet in the American civil rights movement after reading the book "Five Smooth Stones". David felt a sense of purpose and satisfaction with the civil rights cause, much like he had in the military. He found that the grass roots efforts were a good fit for him as opposed to the organized protests side of the movement. Ironically, riot control was one of the specialized skills he had been trained for in the Marines.

Even participation in the noble cause of equal treatment under the law for minorities wasn't enough to fill the personal and spiritual void he felt. By the summer of 1972, he was strung out on hard drugs, in the throes of addiction and spiraling out of control. And then, it happened…. God intervened. He spoke to David in a "visitation", in a manner as undeniable and convincing as the proverbial thunderbolt. God had plans for David, he learned in the encounter; but first, David needed to dig himself out of the hell of addiction.

It was a long, jagged road to recovery and it took about a year. Once David made it to the peak of rehabilitation, he was there for good. There was no looking back.

And those intriguing plans God had for him? They included college, with a degree in anthropology, sociology and religion. Next on the list would be Southeastern Seminary in Wake Forest, North Carolina and, eventually, Duke Divinity School and a pastoral career. These were improbable and unimaginable developments for a former drug addict, who, as a young boy, had once hated school and had no interest whatsoever in the ministry.

While serving as a student pastor at Saint Andrews University in North Carolina, David caught sight of a bright-eyed, beautiful young brunette freshman named Sheila Iley and they soon discovered their shared love of the Lord. Like David, Sheila was brought up in the church with believing parents. Within six months, they were engaged to be married. David was a bit nervous about meeting Sheila's parents, whom he understood were quite conservative. They would probably not be happy about their young daughter quickly marrying a long-haired hippy who rode in on a motorcycle to meet them.

Instead, Sheila's father, who as a young man had attempted to enlist in the military after the attack at Pearl Harbor but was turned down because of a knee infirmity, grasped David's hand strongly. "We really appreciate what you boys did over there (in Vietnam)", his future father-in-law told him. David crumpled inside. He was not used to hearing gratitude for his service.

The young married couple finished out their schooling and started a family within a few years as David pastored various churches. Eventually, he found a position within a mainstream national denomination in the early 1980's. Unfortunately, the same politics that plagued the government during the Vietnam era was alive in the church organization. David was fired after he made decisions that the superiors in the national organization thought were "controversial", such as allowing minorities to guest preach at David's church. Of course, an alternative excuse was given by the church for the dismissal.

David would later carve his own path out back into the ministry as an Evangelical Presbyterian and since 1991, he has been the head pastor of Fellowship of Christ Church. From battling the Vietcong in the trenches of war to combatting substance abuse in the pit of addiction to disputing unfair and un-Christ like racial practices in a national church organization, David has been in the lowest of places, fighting against the strongest of odds. He has been just the kind of guiding light so many hurting and lost souls have needed over the years and he has led countless people to Christ. David is not one to preach platitudes from a lofty altar. He understands the pain of the suffering "forgotten" kinds of people because he has lived it.

At 70, this father of four and grandfather of twelve is still married to his college sweetheart and still preaching away. When his congregation votes to give him a raise, he defers it back to investment in the church. It is now 2018 and one thing that has changed for the better is the country's attitude and acceptance of its veterans. After the war, David often told people that veterans of Vietnam were different than those from other wars. They felt like they could not even recognize Memorial Day or Veteran's Day because how could you participate in holidays that celebrated you when you had spent years trying to suppress and conceal that very same service? As Bob

Dylan once said of that era, "the times, they are- a changing". The culture of appreciation of our veterans has come full circle and as seen in the picture, David fully embraces his military past and yes, he celebrates those holidays that were earned by him. Thank heavens for that and Semper Fi.

"QUICK! SAY A PRAYER"

One of my earliest memories is one day as I was riding to kindergarten with my mother at the wheel. Suddenly, we heard the shrill alarm of an ambulance bearing down on us from behind.

"Quick! Say a prayer!" said Mom as she pulled to the side of the road to let the ambulance pass.

I asked why. At four years old, I was used to saying nightly prayers only for the people I knew.

"You can always pray for anyone you don't know", she explained. "You may not know the person, but God does. Every time you hear a siren, it means someone is in trouble and they need help. So always say a prayer when you hear a siren. Your prayers may be the only ones sent up for that stranger in need."

Mom's wise words stuck. Years later, here I am, a middle-aged wife and mother and I instinctively stop and say a prayer every time I hear a siren, no matter where I am or what I am doing. Over the years, I have added a variation, though. In addition to praying for the person whose need has prompted the siren, I pray for the first responders on the other side of the alarm, coming to aid.

Whether it is a police officer, fireman, armed services personnel or EMT, those who rush into the face of danger instead of away from it are a special breed. Every day, they put their lives on the line to save the rest of us from disaster. September 11, 2001 is but one poignant example of the sacrifice and heroism of the vital group of professionals we refer to as first responders.

"Dear Lord, please aid and comfort those to whom the sirens are delivering help. Embrace their trouble with your healing hands. Fortify and protect the first responders as they approach and assist the people in need. Make clear and unobstructed their paths to the purpose of their work and restore them safely to their families at the end of the day. Amen."

Stephanie Salb

STEPHEN BROOKS

L. Scot "Doc" Folensbee
Diplomatic Security Service
Date of Service - 1985 - 2003
Close friend and colleague

Always a courageous man, Doc fought a lengthy illness with passion and when I was visiting him, usually with a smile and a quick wit. Even in spite some hard days, I am told his sense of humor never faltered and he continued to talk with friends and family from all over the world.

A highly decorated combat medic in Vietnam. He was awarded the Silver Star, two Bronze Stars, and 4 Purple Hearts, along with various Valor Awards for his efforts in battle. Scot was a member of the then highly classified Studies and Observation Group known as SOG in the Military Assistance Command – Vietnam (MAC V) where he earned his nickname "Doc" that would follow him for the into Diplomatic Security Service (DSS) and throughout his career.

When telling Scot of my intent to model the recurring character on him, he was pleased and yet humble. I tried my best to make the character as close to him as possible and he was pleased with the result. The "Warrior Poet" awoke on the pages the same as he was to me personally, Doc Ellersbee was the stabilizing influence that William "Mac" Mackenzie Donovan needed throughout the adventures and occasionally misadventures in the first four books. The Sailing The Curvature of The Earth series.

Scot shared with me he wanted to write a book centered DS and I was only too happy to tell him I would assist him any way I could. Sadly, before he could make much headed way his illness advanced to where he could not proceed. So, this one is for you Brother. I hope you approve and you take it as the one you would have written if you could have.

Thank you for sharing with me a piece of your personality and bigger than life persona. You were, and always be a dedicated DS agent, gentleman of the first order, and a warrior poet. I will always be honored you allowed me into to your circle of friends. I am all the better for it – Thank you Doc Folensbee.

On a Personal Note:
Scot taught me about life that no matter the circumstances, be a gentleman and true to yourself.

I say thank you to my dear friend Scot "Doc" Folensbee by being professional, and a gentleman even when dealing aggressors and those wishing ill upon me and our nation.

Thanks to Scot, I truly believe in service before self.
Stephen Brooks

In Photo, Scot "Doc" Folensbee somewhere in Vietnam

STEVE JENKINS

Thank You Frank!

The term, "war is hell" has many different meanings depending on the person and experience. Today, the term is mostly attributed to Post Traumatic Stress Disorder (PTSD). This disorder comes in many different manifestations and intensities and usually results in dramatic changes in one's life and touches those around the person.

After Vietnam, many suffered PTSD and we had not yet fully realized what it was or what it meant. I personally had friends that returned from the war, who weren't the same person for many different, and at times excruciating reasons. Bodies were changed, minds were altered, and the aftermath was devastating for so many.

I was commissioned as we were pulling out of Vietnam and although I was not deployed, I was impacted in a positive way. I feel like it was the handiwork of God.

I had a friend, we'll call him Frank to protect his identity, that saw the horrors of war as a medic. On Frank's first mission, as he jumped from his Huey medivac helicopter, the first casualty was his best friend from high school. His friend had no chance of making it and passed way in his arms. Think about that for a moment. Let it sink in. What would be your feelings at that moment and moving forward? It affected Frank's life in many ways but in some respects with positive outcomes for Frank and myself.

Frank returned from the war and started work at a state agency then moved on to the private sector. We became friends, and as I worked my way through graduate school, he offered me a job as an intern. It was during that time that I witnessed Frank's compassion for others and his warped sense of humor that kept us all going during those pressure-packed times of the business. We worked with very impoverished communities and I saw Frank's desire to do whatever he could to improve the lives of residents.

Frank married a wonder young lady that understood the horrors that Frank had endured in Vietnam. She stood with him and help with his struggles.

They were blessed with a little baby and things changed for Frank and, as a result, for myself.

One day, I walked into the office and Frank said, "I'm quitting, and it is yours"! What? Frank had reached a realization that the stress of the job exacerbated the fallout of this Vietnam experience and chose to step away. His choice was to become an "at home Dad" which proved to be the best therapy in the world for him.

So, why does this matter? What impact did Frank have on my life? Frank was one of those special individuals that God brings across your path to help mold your destiny. Frank's compassion rubbed off on me in the beginning of my career and is with me to this day. Frank cared more about others than himself which, as I looked back, may have been a coping mechanism. I saw that in our work together in the depressed communities and learned that there are things more important in life than ourselves.

As I moved forward in my career, there was God again! One day I was at a function that was celebrating an economic success in the community I served. I felt a tap on my shoulder and turn to find find a lady with tears in her eyes. She just said, "thank you". When I inquired for what, she said because of the work I did her husband had a job he never dreamed was possible, and they now had the opportunity to own a home.

The interactions with Frank and this lady shaped my approach to my career. That approach was to be a servant leader.

Over the years, I lost track of Frank but realize the profound impact he had on me as a person and my purpose in life. It is so easy to get wrapped up in what we believe the world tells us is important. We all need to take time to reflect on those moments that really matter…holding a dying friend in your arms or seeing the tears of a grateful heart.

Thank you Frank! You mattered in my life!

SOMEBODY, SOMEWHERE IS DEPENDING ON YOU TO DO WHAT GOD HAS CALLED YOU TO DO.

MIKERODRIGUEZ
MikeRodriguezInternational.com

TRACEY NAZARENUS

Nicholas Anthony Ramos

Thirty years ago, I was blessed with a beautiful baby boy named Nicholas Anthony Ramos, and today I'm blessed to be able to share his story. Nic was thoughtful in high school, although sometimes he was thoughtful because there were cute girls in his study group. At 17, Nic joined the Army when most teenagers were enjoying their summer. Writing me from his boot camp in Missouri, he said he regretted not studying harder in school. During his graduation from boot camp, I was in awe of my son, dressed head to toe in camo. After returning home for his senior year, he was restless to complete his schooling early in anticipation for the future. It wasn't long before he left for the Army Medic program. After acclimating to the Army, returning to civilian life left him unfulfilled.

Being in the midst of wars in Iraq and Afghanistan, I flooded with worry. The young man I raised had trained as a Master at Arms. When he was deployed in Afghanistan, all I could do was pray for him and avoid watching the news. I despised when others would remind me of how dangerous it was for Nic, which made it all the more terrifying when he and his unit went missing for two weeks. The letters and calls he made relayed a positive experience; he traveled all throughout Afghanistan and was based in Kandahar and the Bagram Air Force Base, though he saved the scary details.

Upon gaining two weeks leave, Nic traveled across the world to show up at my work. Wearing his camo, he stood outside. I recall seeing a soldier beyond the window that looked just like my son and, as a matter of fact, it was him! On his visit, he surprised each member of the family: his sister at her high school, his dad in his office, and his grandparents at their door. I imagine he felt wonderful for the wealth of excitement we all had during his leave but, of course, he had to return to duty. I was beyond proud of this man of courage and determination, despite my concerns.

When he returned for good, he was pretty banged up but retained his resilience. Within months, at only 25, he was the Captain of a private prison. Regardless of his age, he always earned his respect. He got married, then adopted my grandson, Dominic. Before long, he had adjusted to civilian life, however, after long, memories of war seeped into his mind. He opted for a silent fight, aided by the VA drugs that slated his thoughts and memories. The cost of stopping the nightmares he woke up screaming from was becoming a shell. One night, his wife called me, terrified that Nic might commit suicide.

I had no idea how bad it was until, arriving at his home, I saw my little boy, a grown man, crying into a pillow and telling me he can't live anymore; that he's evil, haunted, and unable to keep the casualties of war out of his head. This prompted me to intensively learn about the effects of PTSD and the drugs that are administered to returning Veterans. With time, the Nic I knew before deployment was coming back. He had divorced but strengthened in the process. He turned his life around with the determination he had in raising his child and the desire to help others with difficult emotions. He went to college and earned a double bachelor in counseling and psychology. Now, my son is a youth services specialist and an extraordinary single dad striving to help others with difficult emotions. Nic is the sweetest, most loving, caring and giving man I've ever met. He is my best friend and confidant.

Nic is also the Exifficio of Crusaders: Valor for Veterans, the nonprofit I started after our experiences. It is truly an honor to tell his story...the courage of my 17-year-old boy, the one who risked his life for this country. Today, he gives everything and everyone every bit of himself. He is Nicolas Anthony Ramos, my son and hero.

Valorforveterans.us
Linkedin: Tracey Nazarenus
FaceBoook: Tracey Nazarenus
www.crusdersequestrian.org

TRISH BUCHANAN

Paul Buchanan
East Hartford Police Department
July 24, 1989 – March 12, 2013
Patrol Officer, Badge #208

East Hartford Police Officer Paul Buchanan, Badge #208, was my best friend, my husband, and the love of my life. Paul and I were best friends – meeting at the age of 17. We were married for almost 29 years; we have two amazing sons, Jared and Benjamin.

March 12, 2013 – was the day I experienced the worst tragedy in my life and since that tragic day, I've been on a journey of pain, grief, sorrow, healing, and love. I never would have imagined that I could have survived without him, but God has a way of taking tragedies and turning them into something good and LOVE has carried me through.

Paul was a kind hearted and beloved police officer who always did his job with truth and integrity and always thought of others. His police career as a patrol officer started in July 1989. During his career he received one Meritorious Service Citation, two Lifesaving Citations, and multiple Commendations. He was East Hartford Police Officer of the year in 2008. His personnel file was filled with all things good and true. He was a friend to all. Others described him as *"A person to always bring a smile to your face; a true leader, respectful to all, honest, selfless; exudes integrity. The type of cop you want to get pulled over by."*

Even in the last moments of his life, he had his law enforcement brothers and sisters on his mind as he wrote in a letter *"...make my death an issue and help others like me."* Little did I know that Paul's message would become my reason for survival, my heart and passion, my mission and purpose for life? Because of his unwavering love for others, my dream, the *"Believe 208"* dream to help our first responders, was born.

After Paul's death, my sons and I knew that we were not going to hide behind what happened to our beloved Paul. I just didn't know, however, how we were going to honor his message. One day, while traveling down the highway, praying and crying, and asking for God's help, I came upon a tractor trailer truck which I was drawn to. On the back were written words, that I was barely able to see. As I came closer I could make out the words and my prayers were answered. *"Believe"* That's all I needed to do was *"Believe"* – Believe that something good would come from Paul's death by suicide. Believe that alone I can do so little; together we can do so much. Just *"Believe"*.

The *"Believe 208"* mission was established in Paul's memory and works collaboratively with Connecticut Alliance to Benefit Law Enforcement (CABLE). CABLE is a non-profit, 501 (C) (3), that brings community and law enforcement resources together to address common issues related to mental health.

With the funds that we have raised with our *"Believe 208" 5K Run for the Brave & Finest"*, we have been able to promote awareness of the importance of physical and emotional well-being for our first responders by providing peer support training; training for mental health clinicians who wish to provide mental health services to police and their families; created a directory of vetted and trained clinicians who are specially trained to work with officers and their families; and provided a *"Mindfitness"* Training Retreat. Also, we have been able to provide resources and referrals to law enforcement officers, given grocery store gift cards to law enforcement officers in need, paid medical insurance deductibles to help officers get into treatment programs, and have helped family survivors of police suicide.

It's often through tragedies that you find your voice they say. For me, Paul has help me find the voice of truth in a once taboo and silent subject. The subject of police suicide. Suicide – a terrible, horrible, ugly, and hidden word. Yet, because of Paul's death, lives have been saved, silence has been broken, and we are on the verge of changing laws in Connecticut to help our first responders.

My love for Paul remains forever. He has helped me change from a quiet, humble, "afraid to speak in public" person to an outspoken advocate for all our first responders. He has taught me how to be a friend to all and to *"Believe"* that a person can move mountains by carrying away small stones. It may seem impossible, but each and every step counts. Today, I am a better and stronger person because of my beloved husband's love and message.

Even in his death, he is still saving lives. I shall never forget my #208 and all those lost to suicide. It is not how they died, but how they lived.
Trish Buchanan

Facebook: Believe 208: Run for the Brave & Finest
believe208run@gmail.com
@Believe208

UNFORGETTABLE FACES & STORIES
YOUR STORY TOLD BY YOU.

 www.facebook.com/
unforgettablefacesandstories

 instagram.com/EileenDoyon

 twitter.com/FacesandStories

 www.youtube.com/user/
FacesandStories

 www.pinterest.com/
facesandstories

Thank you for purchasing Patriots of Courage: Tributes to First Responders!

Other books in the Unforgettable Faces & Stories series:
Starting Over: Stories of New Beginnings
The Second My Life Changed Forever
Letters To Heaven
Pet Tales: Unconditional Love
Best Friends: Forever & Ever
Keepsakes: Treasures From The Heart
Dedications: Dads & Daughters

Thank you again for your support! We would love for you to participate in one of our upcoming books...YOUR story told by YOU!

REVIEWS

The Second My Life Changed Forever

By AE on August 27, 2016: A wonderful book and inspiring author! Each story is an act of hope, courage, and incredible strength. The book is written with immense love and a testament to the human spirit! It gives each of us promise that even in the most difficult of times, there is hope .Thank you, Eileen Doyon, for the beautiful book and the wisdom and life lessons in your every chapter.

July 11, 2016: I really love the idea of so many short stories in one book. Real stories. It's gives the customer an opportunity to read many stories and gives everyone an opportunity to share theirs. Great job!

By B. S. Leidy on July 8, 2016: GREAT READ! Just got my copy today and I can't put it down! Anyone who has lived can appreciate the poignancy of the many stories of personal, and intimate, changes in life. I highly recommend this book!

July 28, 2016: I have now read three of Eileen's books and love them all! I usually read at night time and know I will be up extra late when I read her books. I keep wanting to read the next story and the next story and the next story! Thanks Eileen for inspiring us and sharing "real life" stories! I know this book just came out, but I'm already excited to hear what's next! If you haven't read any of Eileen's books, please do - you'll be glad you did!

By Edward Brewster on January 19, 2017: This is a must read for anyone who has enjoyed the Unforgettable Faces and Stories series by Eileen Doyon. This installment brings the reader back into the world of everyday people, and how life can change in a blink of an eye and how to adjust to those changes and come out on top. These are stories that will inspire and fill you with hope and inspiration. These are not made up or out of someones' imagination They are real. As real as the people who wrote them. I highly suggest this book and series as it will fill you with hope and love and maybe, just maybe they can help you find your way through the struggles of life.

July 6, 2016: Who doesn't need a bit of understanding and compassion as we deal with our daily struggles? This book keeps it real and exemplifies what it means to keep on livin' through all that we encounter. What a blessing!

By Jeanne Buesser on July 21, 2016: A must read! Eileen, I love the book. Your choices of stories are a really nice mix. It was inspiring reading all of them. When we go through hard times we all have to face our demons and not realize the strength we all have to be able to do it. Also that it is when we are in despair or at our lowest point is when the answers come the power to change ourselves and the direction. We may not realize this at that time, or get an aha moment until afterwards when we are able to breathe again,appreciating the opportunity afterwards in hindsight until much later.

July 6, 2016: It completely amazes me the struggles that we face can transform us to something incredibly great and we all have a true purpose. The book is truly inspirational. It completely amazes me the struggles that we face can transform us to something incredibly great and we all have a true purpose in life to inspire each other. I recommend this book to everyone to read especially those who are suffering in life, you can overcome it and inspire others yourself. A MUST READ!!!

By Cory B Houser on July 8, 2016: Eileen did an amazing job capturing the beauty and devastation in the world. People who's second changed them and made them do more good. People who's second opened their eyes and their hearts. This book is full of beauty and courage and love. Thank you for pulling so many of us together to share our second that it all changed.

July 7, 2016: Inspirational and Moving! Thank you so much to Eileen for including me in this book. Having the chance to read other people's experiences, was amazing for me as well. This book includes a lot of inspirational people and life-changing moments. I feel like, once you start reading, it pulls you in!

August 22, 2016: Inspiring. Read it all at once, or one inspiring story a day.... Gift this book to others and share the hope and wonder of these beautiful souls. Eileen did a fabulous job collaborating all these unforgettable true stories!

July 12, 2016: I love everything about this book! What a great idea to let people tell their own story, in their words! Amazing idea, great stories, inspiring people! Kudos Eileen!

By Carrie on June 23, 2016 ~ Inspiring!!!!

By Katy on July 12, 2016: This book is truly an inspiration! In a world of such tragedy, it is amazing to read how people have overcome any obstacle that has come their way.

July 6, 2016: I hope my story will inspire you. Inspiring, heartbreaking, failures, successes, love, passion, vulnerability and so much more. Must read. Buy one for you and gift one.

July 8, 2016: This book is a must have for anyone who has ever faced lose or the threat of losing someone. A Must Have Read! You wont regret it!

By DBB on July 24, 2016: Well done! So many great stories and so well told. Thank you, Eileen, for this literary contribution to the collective soul.

By Ken C. on June 25, 2016: Inspiring. An author that captures peoples amazing stories and inspires each of us.. Thank you for such a great book!

By MJC on July 8, 2016: Beautiful! Beautiful stories to uplift and encourage you. Thank you Eileen for such a wonderful collection!

July 12, 2016: A Heart-wrenching , triumphant, joyous and real roller coaster ride from beginning to end.

By AE on August 27, 2016: A Beautiful Book & One To Be Shared & Gifted. A wonderful book and inspiring author! Each story is a act of hope, courage, and incredible strength. The book is written with immense love and a testament to the human spirit! It gives each of us promise that even in the most difficult of times, there is hope .Thank you, Eileen Doyon, for the beautiful book and the wisdom and life lessons in your every chapter.

By Soulsis on July 3, 2016 Great book, uplifting! Good collection of stories to inspire and teach.

July 7, 2016: Just incredible! Just perfect life stories. Heartbreaking.

Letters To Heaven

By Mary Potter Kenyon on May 21, 2017

A wonderful compilation of letters to loved ones who died. A great idea for anyone who wishes there was something they had said; write a letter to your loved one. Then bury it in the cemetery, like I did, or burn it. Writing is healing, either way.

By Julie Morse on June 20, 2017

These stories brought back feelings of the deep love I felt for relatives who have moved on. Everyone has a story and these ones were told beautifully.

By M Hallon June 19, 2017

I highly recommend all of Eileen Doyon's books. Eileen is a breath of fresh air. She is a very talented writer....we all have a story. I bought every single book she has written.

Please refer to Eileen Doyon's Author page on Amazon.com (www.amazon. com/Eileen-Doyon/e/B00J8WTHW8) for additional reviews on all books

This is a "Thank You First Responders" special section that we wanted to add to this book and share with all of you.

What do kids think of when they hear "First Responders"? There are big shoes to fill in the years ahead. Please read these wonderful "Thank Yous" from the 3rd Grade Class of Fort Edward, New York, my hometown. A special thank you to both teachers, Mrs. Bump and Mrs. Smatko. Also, thank you to Vicki Plude of the Fort Edward Free Library in your help with my T-Shirt program, kids helping kids. You can visit my website for details! www.unforgettablefacesandstories.com/tafr-tshirts

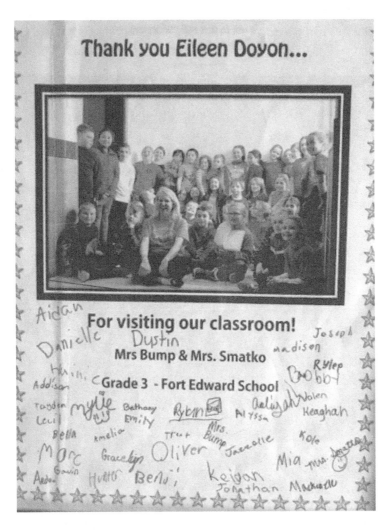

Puts other people's lives in front of their own

Outstanding service

Listens to the Chief

Is kind and respectful

Calm

Ends peoples' days well and makes them feel safe inside!

First responders are here to stay,
They are here every night and day,
They save people's lives and, RISK THEIR OWN!
First responders will save people TODAY!

First to help
In the day and night they encourage and educate people
Really brave
Super caring
Teaching people to be safe, helping when they get a call
Really helpful
Encouraging
Selfless
Paramedics help get people to hospitals
Officers patrol the city to make sure we're safe and we don't get hurt
Never do they give up
Do helpful things to help people no matter what, all the time.
Every day they are loyal
Respectful to everyone
Saving people all the time!

Heroic people

Everyone thanks them

R

Overcoming obstacles to save lives

Emergency helpers

Saving people's lives!

Thank You First Responders!!!

Police officers are first responders. I want to thank all of the police officers for their hard work and for keeping us safe from danger. I especially want to thank the Fort Edward Police Department for keeping our school safe from gun threats and for keeping the town safe from bad guys. Chief Derway and his officers are the best at keeping Fort Edward a safe place to live. We love you guys!!!!!!. **Thank you!!!!!!!!!!!!!!!**

My Aunt Debbie is a nurse at the St. Francis Hospital. She helps people when they are in need or injured. She inspires me because she helps keep people healthy in her community. Aunt Debbie even sometimes help babies. I want to thank her for her hard work. She never gives up no matter what happens. She always does her very best. If you go to the hospital in Poughkeepsie, NY remember to thank my aunt for all she does and know your in great hands!

My aunt is a nurse!

I'd like to say thank you to all first responders for being so brave, helpful, and caring. You risk your life for others even though it's dangerous and risky. You are brave because you put your life at risk. You help people feel better and encourage us with all your helpful words. Thank you for helping us first responders!

Police Officer

I would thank the Fort Edward Police Department for arresting the criminals and saving us from them. The police in Fort Edward are nice and helpful. I like meeting them and having them visit my school.

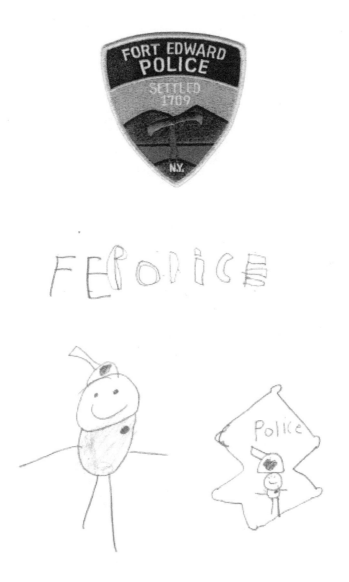

I would like to thank my Mom and Dad
for being first responders. My mother is a nurse. She
works at a hospital, and she is very important to many
people but especially me! My father is a corrections officer
and a volunteer firefighter. I'm happy that they are both
first responders because they help the community stay
safe and healthy. My Dad has fought big fires and my
Mom helps save lives everyday. I love my my first
responders! How about you?

I'd like to say Thank You to all first responders for being so so brave and selfless. Even when you're taking a risk and and when things are dangerous you still help others. Firefighters are brave because they put out fires and save the lives of others. E.M.T. save the lives of others by helping them even when they have broken their bones. Our military fight in wars and they protect us too. Lifeguards save us when we are drowning. I'd just like to say THANK YOU to all first responders for protecting us from a lot of dangers and helping us by risking your lives.

Doctor

I'd like to say THANK YOU to all first responders for being so courageous, encouraging, and calm. I would also like to mention a few first responders in my family, my grandma, and pop- pop are EMT's, my papa was in the Marines but, I never got to meet him. Thank you for all that you do first responders and for putting our lives first!

First coming to a emergency
In our communities
Risking everything to save lives
Showing others you care
Trying to help you

Respecting others
Educating kids
Saving people in a situation
Paramedics
Oh so brave
Never giving up
Everyone feeling safe
Responds first

police man

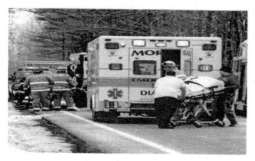

I want to thank the ambulance workers for helping my brother when he had two seizures and my dad when he had one seizure. My dad had one because he was working outside and it was really hot. He did not drink any water the whole day. My brother had two because his temperature was high and while he was sleeping. When you see a ambulance worker, make sure you thank them for all the wonderful things they do.

I would like to thank **Officer Walkins** for everything that he has done for me and my family. I want to thank him for making me feel safe when my step dad went to jail. **Officer Walkins** and the other officers made me not feel so scared. I would like to thank them all.

I would like to thank the Fort Edward Volunteer Firefighters that keep my Ford Edward community safe. If there was a fire at my school, they would be rushing to the school to save us. They come to are school to teach fire safety. I'm glad we have first responders in our town!!! I had breakfast at the firehouse too!!! They volunteer to save us and risk their lives.

First one there

*I*s a hero

*R*esponds first

*S*elfless

*T*hey are courageous!

*R*espectful

*E*ncouraging

*S*o helpful

*P*aramedic

*O*h so brave

*N*ear by

*D*etermined

*E*ducate others

*R*escue people

(Mini) Army man

I would like to thank all first responders because they serve our country and keep it safe for all people. First responders like EMT's, firefighters, police officers, army men and women and many others risk their own lives for the rest of us. You should always thank first responders. They help, serve, and care.

My Pa

I would like to thank my Pa who was a first responder. He was in the Marines in a war called Vietnam. Vietnam was the bloodiest war america has ever faced. Someone threw a grenade at my Pa. It blasted him back into a wall, but he survived the blast. He did hurt his leg very badly. His leg didn't heal until a few years ago. Thank you Pa for protecting our country!

I will like to thank the EMT's in my community. .My principal, Mrs.Jones, is an EMT. She keeps people safe when they are hurt. She is also great at doing her job every day and still finds time to volunteer to help in emergencies. I want to thank her for keeping the kids at school healthy and safe. I also want to thank her for being a great EMT. Mrs. Jones inspires me to be safe and want to help others. When you see an EMT make sure you thank him or her. If you see Mrs. Jones, please thank her for being a GREAT principal and EMT!

Paramedic

I want to thank police men and women in Fort Edward. They took my sister's boyfriend out because he was mean and rude to my sister. They are great first responders.

I would to thank first responders with this quadlet

First Responders saving the day
Risking their life while they are at bay.
When people need help they will be there
They will be on time....... that they can spare.

A first responder is oh so very brave,
We thank them all for the lives they save
They help us when we have an emergency,
For being so kind, helpful and …..showing bravery.

First to come to the rescue

In our community

Responds all the time

Stays clam

Thank You

Right at the emergency

Ever so helpful

Self less

Putting other people first

Outstanding Service

Never give up

Deserves respect

Encouraging to others

Responsibility

Situations get solved!

(Mini) Aarmy man

I'd like to thank a first responder by writing this poem:

Helps people in need

Encourages others

Responds first to emergencies

Outstanding community member

Thank You First Responders!

I'd like to thank a first responder with this poem

They are so Helpful

And Encouraging

They are also Respectful

And Oh so kind

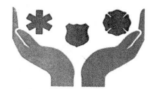

I would like to thank my uncle, Police Chief Justin Derway, because he is a police officer in my community. Once there was a threat at my school. He came and made us feel safe and protected. He came to my classroom and talked to us and let us ask him questions. I am proud that my uncle is the chief. A long time ago my papa was a police officer, but that was before I was born. Police officers are very brave, kind, and caring. They are very brave because if they have a job to do and it is dangerous they still do it. They are kind and caring because they help us when we need it. If you see Chief Derway say thank you!!!

Beyond helpful to people

Risking their lives for other people's lives

Always there when people need help

Very calm during an emergency

Encouraging to others!

Nurses

I would like to thank first responder Chief Derway of the Fort Edward Police Department. Chief Derway is a policeman in Fort Edward and he walks around our school sometimes to make sure everyone is safe. He is a kind and helpful person. I like when he comes to my school making sure everyone was safe. I also like how he came into our classroom. I really like how he has all of that stuff on his uniform. When he came into our classroom he made me feel safe. That is the first responder I'd like to thank.

I would to thank the police officers all over the United States. The police catch a lot of criminals to protect the country. I thank you police officers for helping keep us safe.

If your school is interested in participating in our next book, please contact us at unforgettablefacesandstories@gmail.com. We will do our best to accommodate you.

Made in the USA
Columbia, SC
17 September 2018